BiTE
of
SEATTLE
C👁👁k
b👁👁k

volume VII

Judith Deak
Gretchen Flickinger
Publishers

Gretchen Flickinger
Cover Design, Production

Abraxas Typesetting
Typesetting

Overlake Press
Printing

Dee Cundy
Inspiration

Table of Contents

Dedicated To
Rose Deak and Connie Flickinger
Two Fine Cooks

ADRIATICA
CUCINA MEDITERRANEA

1107 Dexter Ave. N.
Seattle, Washington 98109
(206) 285-5000

Adriatica is located in a remodeled 1920's stucco house on a hill above the south end of Lake Union. Now entering our 13th year, we were just included in *Conde Nast Traveler* Magazine's top 50 restaurants in the U.S. Chef Nancy Flume has been presiding over the kitchen for 10 years, where she prepares an array of Mediterranean dishes. Adriatica is open seven nights 5:30 – 10:00 Sunday through Thursday, until 11:00 Friday & Saturday. Our upstairs lounge serves lighter fare every night until 11:00.

Whole Roasted Garlic

Serves 8

8 heads garlic
¾ c virgin olive oil
⅛ c water
¼ stick butter, melted

rosemary
thyme
other herbs as desired

Preheat oven to 325°.

Peel outer paper off of the heads of garlic, leaving the cloves intact. Trim ¼" off tops (not roots) of garlic.

Place in a baking pan just large enough to hold the garlic with cut side up.

Pour over garlic: olive oil, water, melted butter. Lay a few sprigs of rosemary and thyme on top, or any other herbs you'd like to use (including peppercorns, whole dried chilies...), depending on what flavor you want. Dried herbs are fine – just use less.

Cover pan tightly with foil or lid. Bake 1½ hours or until garlic is very soft when you squeeze it.

Serve warm with croutons, crusty bread and soft cheese – chevre is best! Save oil to dip bread in!

Save oil to dip bread in!

Grilled Pork Tenderloin
with Port & Dried Cranberry Sauce

Serves 6

6 pork tenderloins, about 8 oz ea,
  trimmed of all fat
1 c olive oil
3 cloves garlic, minced
1 tsp black pepper
1 Tbsp fresh thyme or 1 tsp dried

Cranberry Sauce ingredients:
1 fifth ruby port
1 pt heavy cream
1 Tbsp minced shallots
1 tsp black pepper
½ tsp thyme
½ c sun-dried cranberries

Make a marinade for the pork tenderloins of the olive oil, garlic, pepper and thyme. Let marinate four to six hours, or overnight.

Charcoal-grill tenderloins, turning on all sides until medium (just a little pink), about 10 minutes.

To prepare sauce: in medium saucepan, reduce port over high heat to 1 cup. Add other ingredients except for cranberries and reduce over low heat until sauce starts to thicken. Add cranberries and continue to thicken sauce. Serve immediately with tenderloins.

Warm Cabbage Salad
with Walnuts & Chevre

Serves 2

½ head red cabbage, cut in
julienne
1 sm red onion, julienne
1 bunch watercress, stems removed
2 shallots, minced

½ tsp ground black pepper
4 oz bacon, chopped & browned
4 oz walnuts, toasted
1½ Tbsp walnut oil
4 Tbsp balsamic vinegar

Toss cabbage and red onion together.

In large saute pan, heat the walnut oil over medium high heat. Add shallots, pepper and bacon. As shallots start to soften, add cabbage and toss well. Add vinegar, toss, then add walnuts and watercress, toss again. Serve immediately with chevre crumbled over top.

4

Adriatica Curried Mussels

Serves 6-8 as appetizer

3 Tbsp butter
½ lg onion, chopped
1 Tbsp minced garlic
½ tsp ground cumin
½ tsp crushed red chilies
½ tsp turmeric
pinch ground clove

½ tsp ground black pepper
¼ tsp salt
2 tomatoes, chopped
2 lbs cleaned mussels
1 c dry white wine
¼ lemon, juiced
1 bunch cilantro, chopped

Saute onion and garlic in butter until golden. Add all spices, cook 2-3 minutes, until aromatic.

Add the mussels, tomato and wine. Stir well, cover and steam until all mussels are open, about 3-5 minutes.

Add lemon juice and cilantro, toss well, serve immediately.

ALI BABA

707 E. Pine
Seattle, Washington 98122
(206) 325-2299

Ali Baba Restaurant is a pioneer in Middle Eastern cuisine. You might say that Ali Baba Restaurant is the grand-daddy of all the Middle Eastern restaurants in the Seattle metropolitan area.

For the past twenty years Ali Baba has prided itself in offering exquisite dishes that are prepared and served in an atmosphere of professionalism.

The restaurant, family owned and operated, takes great pride in the preparation of its unique cuisine which is not only pleasing to the palate but extremely healthy.

Baba Kannoug

Serves 2-4

1 lg eggplant   1 clove garlic
½ c tahini   juice of 3 lemons
2 Tbsp oil   salt to taste

Bake eggplant at 500° until tender. Split open and scoop out the inside pulp and the juices.

Mix and mash tahini, lemon juice, garlic and salt to make tahini sauce. Add mashed eggplant and mix.

Place on platter and pour oil on top. Garnish with parsley and tomato slices, if desired.

Shawarma Chicken

Serves 2

1 *whole, boneless chicken breast,*
  sliced in strips
one onion, sliced
one tomato, sliced
one green pepper, sliced in strips
hot spices (special)

salt
⅛ *tsp allspice*
1 *clove garlic, crushed*
½ *lemon, juiced*
vegetable oil

Marinate chicken slices with garlic and lemon juice.

Saute chicken with vegetables in oil. Then add the salt and the allspice. Serve with rice.

Amity Vineyards
18150 Amity Vineyards S.E.
Amity, Oregon 97101
(503) 835-2362

Soupe au Vin
Wine & Vegetable Soup

Serves 8

2 lg onions (Walla Walla Sweet or Yellow)

3 carrots, peeled and diced

3 pink turnips or one lg yellow one (parsnips, Yellow Finnish potatoes may be substituted)

2 med red peppers, diced

2 leeks, white part only

2 Tbsp butter or margarine

1 Tbsp olive oil

2 c Amity Pinot Noir + 1 glass for cook

1½ qts chicken broth (I use low sodium)

1 Tbsp arrowroot or cornstarch

2 Tbsp chives, minced

salt

fresh ground pepper

Schilling Mixed Pepper as garnish

Preparation time about 45 minutes from start to finish for a wonderful homemade soup, low in sodium and saturated fats.

Saute the vegetables in the butter and oil over medium heat for 3-5 minutes, stirring occasionally until barely soft. Add wine and bring to boil, uncovered. Simmer for 20 minutes. Add the broth. Simmer for 10 minutes more, stir. Dissolve the arrowroot in 3 tablespoons of water, then stir it into the soup. Simmer for 3 minutes, sprinkle with chives and garnish with croutons if desired and serve.

Le Regal Aille
A Garlic Treat

Serves 8

6 Tbsp olive oil

6 Tbsp sweet butter

50 garlic cloves, peeled

1½ c Amity Estate Dry Riesling
  or for a fuller treat,
  Amity Gewurtztraminer

8 slices toasted bread

8 Tbsp minced basil or parsley
  and chives

fresh ground pepper

Heat oil and butter in a heavy skillet and saute the garlic for 5 minutes. Add wine and pepper to garlic and simmer for 15 minutes, uncovered. Transfer cooked garlic to food processor or crush with a fork until a paste is formed. Spread garlic paste on toast.

Quickly reduce wine sauce left from cooking garlic at least by half. Pour sauce over toast, sprinkle with basil or parsley and chives and serve.

Enjoy with rest of wine.

BITE OF INDIA

Crossroads Shopping Center
15600 NE 8th, Suite 9
Bellevue, Washington 98006
(206) 643-4263

Many people like us have come from the Southern part of India, and those who have tried South Indian cuisine feel there is a real need for an authentic south Indian restaurant in the Greater Seattle area. The South Indian cuisine differs from the familiar North Indian Cuisine not only in the menu, but also in some of the spices used in preparing various curries.

The Bite of India opened four years ago, offers South Indian cuisine, and has become very popular. The menu is prepared from Mrs. Usha Reddy's Family recipes.

The food is healthy because no additives or preservatives are used, and 100% vegetable oils are used in cooking. There are many popular vegetarian and non-vegetarian dishes on the menu. One of the best liked menu items is Dosas, 100% vegetarian, spicy, delicious and exotic! Over 45,000 Dosas have been served since Bite of India opened.

Bite of India offers Indian home cooking at its best!

Chicken Curry

Serves 2

1 lb boneless chicken breast
2 Tbsp vegetable oil
1 med onion, chopped
3 cloves garlic and 2" pc fresh
    ginger root, minced together
Grind together:
2 cloves
2 cardamom (whole)

1" stick cinnamon
2 Tbsp slivered almonds
¼ tsp cayenne pepper
⅛ tsp ground turmeric
1 tsp ground coriander
salt to taste
½ c plain yogurt
½ c water

Preparation time is about 30 minutes.

Wash and dry chicken with paper towel. Cut into bite-sized pieces. Heat oil in 2 quart pan over medium heat. Add onion and saute for 2 minutes. Add ginger-garlic paste and saute for 1 minute.

Reduce the temperature to medium-low. Add all the spices and yogurt one by one, stirring after each addition, and saute for 2 minutes. Add chicken and stir well so that the chicken is coated with spice mixture. Leave on low for 5 minutes, stirring occasionally.

Increase the heat to medium-high and cook for another 5 minutes, stirring often. Then add water and cook for an additional 10 minutes.

Serve with plain or fried rice. If more gravy is needed, add ½ cup of water and cook for an additional 5 to 10 minutes.

Vegetable Fried Rice

Serves 4

1 c Basamathi rice
¼ c vegetable oil
½ stick cinnamon
3 cloves (whole)
3 cardamoms (whole)

1 sm onion, chopped
1 c sliced carrots, fresh or frozen
1 c cut green beans, fresh or frozen
1½ c water
salt to taste

Clean, wash and soak the rice for ½ hour. Heat oil in 2 quart pan. Add cinnamon, cloves, cardamom and onions. Saute until light brown. Add vegetables and cook for 3 to 5 minutes.

Then add water and salt. Bring to a boil. Drain rice completely and add to the boiling water. Cook for 3 minutes on medium heat. Reduce the heat and cook until rice is done.

Rahitha

Makes approximately ¾ cup

½ c plain yogurt (low or non-fat)   ⅛ tsp black pepper
½ cucumber, peeled, seeds
  removed, and chopped

Blend yogurt to smooth consistency with fork. Then add chopped cucumber, salt, pepper and mix well. Serve with fried rice.

Curry: a blend of many spices, such as coriander, cinnamon, cumin, cardamom, cloves, ginger, garlic and turmeric. Rahitha: seasoned yogurt.

Purchase specialty ingredients at: R & M Videos & Spices (526-1793); Singh International Videos & Spices (643-0366); Shanti Videos & Spices (228-9659); Souk's Spices, Public Market.

12000 Bel-Red Road
Bellevue, Washington 98005
(206) 454-0600

Brenner Brothers Baking Co has been a Northwest tradition since 1902. In the early days devoted customers rode the trolley car up Yesler Way to buy fresh baked goods and visit with Abe Brenner and the Brenner family. Abe passed away in 1953 and sons Itsey, Charlie and Joe took over the business, moving to East Cherry and Empire Way. The brothers moved to Bellevue in the late 60's.

Today grandsons David and Alan (sons of Itsey and Charlie) are carrying on the family business, using the same family recipes and honoring the same traditions.

The Brenner Brothers Bakery & Delicatessen features a full line of breads, pastries and delicatessen items, as well as a restaurant and kosher bakery.

Water Bagels

Makes 18

cornmeal
1 ¼-oz pkg active dry yeast
3 Tbsp sugar
1 c warm water (110°F)
2 tsp salt

2 Tbsp vegetable oil
½ c gluten flour (hard wheat flour)
3½ c white flour

Dust baking sheet with cornmeal. Combine yeast and 1 Tbsp sugar in large bowl. Pour ½ cup warm water over the mixture. Let stand until yeast has dissolved and is bubbly. Add remaining ½ cup water. Add 1 Tbsp of sugar, salt, oil and gluten flour. Beat thoroughly. Add white flour, stirring until firm and well blended. (If dough is firm before all flour is added, add remaining flour during kneading.)

Turn dough out on lightly floured board. Knead vigorously for 10 minutes. Divide into 18 equal pieces. Form into bagels by rolling into cylinders and fusing the ends.
Put bagels on prepared baking sheet in a warm, draft-free place. Let rise 20 to 30 minutes.

Ten minutes before bagels are finished rising, bring 3 to 4 qts water to boil in large stockpot or Dutch oven. Preheat oven to 400 degrees F.

Add remaining sugar to boiling water. Drop 3 bagels into water. Bagels should stay on surface. If bagels do not pop immediately to surface, they have not risen enough. Poach each side of bagel 2 minutes. After poaching each bagel, remove with slotted spoon and transfer to cornmeal baking sheet. Lightly dust with cornmeal.

Bake in preheated oven for about 30 minutes or until perfectly brown.

Cabbage Roll

Makes 35

6 to 8 med heads cabbage
5 lbs ground beef
1 onion, diced
3 eggs
1 c rice (uncooked)
1 c tomato juice
⅔ c Matzo Meal
2 Tbsp salt
pepper to taste
½ tsp garlic

2 tsp lemon juice
Sauce:
4 cans tomato juice
2 c tomato sauce
1 c ketchup
1 Tbsp lemon juice
1 Tbsp salt
pepper to taste
1 c sugar

Cook cabbage heads (6 to 8) in boiling water until soft. Prepare meat filling while cabbage cools. Roll palm-size meat filling in cabbage. Place rolled cabbage in pan with sauce. Place in oven for 3½ hours at 325 degrees, and serve.

Matzo Ball Soup

Serves 30

22 eggs
2 Tbsp salt
½ tsp pepper

1 lb Matzo Meal
homemade chicken broth

Boil water in a large saucepan with 1 Tbsp of chicken base. Put salt and pepper in bowl. Add eggs and beat lightly. Add Mazto Meal. Let sit for 15 minutes, no longer.

Get a small bowl of water, wet hands. Put one Tbsp of Matzo Meal mix in your hands, roll in balls and drop in pot of boiling water until all is finished. Cook for 45 to 50 minutes. Let cool.

Add to broth just before serving.

Note: do not start mixing ingredients until water is boiling.

F café ORZA!

festive italian

122 South Jackson
Seattle, Washington 98104
(206) 622-8908

Tequila Chicken Fettucine

Serves 4

½ c olive oil
1½ lbs boneless chicken breast
6 cloves garlic, chopped
4 oz red pepper
4 oz green pepper
2 limes, juiced

1½ oz cilantro
½ tsp salt
½ tsp pepper
½ c tequila
1½ c heavy cream
24 oz fettucine, cooked and hot

Dice chicken into ½" cubes.

Heat oil and brown chicken with garlic. Add red and green peppers and brown. Add tequila and burn off. Add cilantro, salt, pepper and juice of both limes. Combine well.

Pour in heavy cream. Bring sauce to boil until thickened. Toss sauce with fettucine noodles and serve.

CAFELOC

407 Broad Street
Seattle, Washington
(206) 441-6883

Center House
Seattle Center
(206) 728-9292

Cafe Loc is a family owned restaurant which was opened in 1978 at 407 Broad Street. In two years this location had to be greatly enlarged to accommodate more customers during lunch and dinner.

In 1981 a fast food operation featuring the most popular Cafe Loc dishes was opened in the Seattle Center House. Both locations continue to receive excellent reviews from restaurant critics throughout the Puget Sound area.

A veteran food vendor at numerous street fairs since 1978, Cafe Loc is well known at the University Street Fair, Folklife Festival, Fremont Fair, Heritage Festival, Bite of Seattle, and Bumbershoot.

Cafe Loc continues to provide quality ethnic foods at reasonable prices.

Sweet & Sour Chicken

Serves 2

1 chicken breast, boned and cut into strips

1 sm onion, cut into bite size pieces

½ med green pepper, cut into bite size pieces

1 carrot, cut into bite size pieces

2 tsp vegetable oil

8 pineapple chunks

Sweet & Sour sauce mixture:

¼ c of sugar

¼ c of pineapple juice

¼ c tomato paste or ketchup

2½ Tbsp vinegar

1 Tbsp cornstarch to thicken the sauce

In 2 Tbsp cooking oil, stir fry onion and chicken until chicken is done. Add green pepper, carrots, pineapple chunks and mix well. Add sweet and sour sauce and cook until thickened.

Serve hot with steamed rice.

Cafe Sophie

1921 First Avenue, Butterworth Building
Seattle, Washington 98101
(206) 441-6139

In 1903 the Butterworth Building was constructed to house the Butterworth Mortuary. Ninety years later it is the site of one of Seattle's most intriguing restaurants. Cafe Sophie was ten years of collecting, dreaming and designing by its founder Shane Dennis. Dennis wanted to create a grand European style bistro, reminiscent of those he enjoyed on this travels through Europe.

Cafe Sophie stands as the culmination of his dreams. Whether it is dining underneath the broad stone porticoes on the sidewalk as the bustle of First Avenue passes by, or coffee and pastry in the Bistro, you might just have to remind yourself that you are not in Paris. Once serving as the funeral parlors chapel, The Grand Salon dining room has high cathedral ceilings where baroque angels and stone gargoyles gaze down at diners through a forest of gilt and mirrors. Request one of the private booths and draw the heavy emerald green velvet curtains for guaranteed intimacy. Tucked in back of the restaurant is the Library with book-lined redwalls, fireplace and impressive view of Elliott Bay. Intimate dining is a specialty at Cafe Sophie and it is considered one of the city's most romantic restaurants.

With the Pike Place Market literally in his back yard, Chef De Cuisine Leonard Reded has at his fingertips the bounty of the Pacific Northwest and his menus reflect that, changing seasonally, often weekly. Reded uses only the finest and freshest of local ingredients to create his dishes. The cuisine is contemporary Northwest steeped in classical European tradition with an eye towards health. Signature dishes include Roast King Salmon with Pinot Noir and Black Mustard Sauce, and Galantine of Duck with a Reduction of Black Muscat and Nectarines. Cafe Sophie's desserts are legendary. European trained pastry chefs work to produce an ever-changing array, from huge confections of mousse and chocolate curls to simple fruit desserts and sorbets.

Citrus Cake
with Summer Berries & Pommegranite Cream

Makes 1 cake

Citrus Cake ingredients:

1 stick unsalted butter, softened

1½ c sugar

5 eggs

5 oz heavy whipping cream

2½ c cake flour, sifted (not self-rising)

1 tsp baking powder

½ tsp lemon zest

½ tsp orange zest

1 Tbsp rum

Pommegranite Cream ingredients:

1 c whipping cream

1 c creme fraiche or sour cream

2 oz lime juice

2 oz honey

1 oz pommegranite grenadine*

fresh strawberries, raspberries, blackberries, etc.

To prepare citrus cake: preheat oven to 350 degrees. Line two 2¼x3½x8" pans with parchment paper. In bowl of mixer with the paddle attachment, cream together sugar and softened butter, until light and fluffy. With machine running on slow speed, add eggs one at a time, letting each one incorporate before adding the next. Add the whipped cream in a slow steady stream. Add the zests and rum. Add the flour and baking powder. Mix.

Pour mixture into prepared pans. Set pans side by side on a cookie sheet and bake on middle rack of oven about 30-35 minutes. Let cool completely before removing from pans.

To prepare Pommegranite Cream: in mixing bowl, combine whipping cream and creme fraiche. Whip until light. Add the honey, grenadine and lime juice to mixture.

Line plates with slices of cake, top with berries and pommegranite cream.

Note: Pommegranite Grenadine is available at specialty foods stores such as Delaurenti's.

Smoked Chicken Salad
with Summer Greens & Blackberries in Hazelnut Dressing

Serves 4

Hazelnut dressing:

¼ c cider vinegar

2 tsp honey

1 tsp grain mustard

1 tsp chopped garlic

½ tsp shallot

1 egg yolk

¾ c olive oil

¼ c hazelnut oil

1 tsp chopped parsley

salt

pepper

For Salad:

1 smoked chicken, 2-2½ lbs

1 pt blackberries

1 lb summer greens (lolla rossa, oak leaf, mizuna, arrugula, frisse)

2 oz roasted hazelnuts

4-6 oz hazelnut dressing

To prepare dressing: in bowl, combine vinegar, honey, mustard, garlic, shallot and egg yolk. Whisk together. Add salt and pepper. Slowly whisk in olive oil, hazelnut oil and parsley. you can also follow the same procedure using a food processor for excellent results.

To prepare salad: debone chicken and shred it into little strips. Set aside. Roast hazelnuts in a hot oven for about seven minutes. Wash your greens and pat or spin dry. Toss with the dressing. Top with chicken, hazelnuts and blackberries.

Note: I get my smoked chicken from Cyril at Seattle Super Smoke. He has, in my opinion, the best around. I generally use locally grown greens from the small farmers in the market. Hazelnut oil is available at Delaurenti's in the market, or any specialty food store.

29

2212 1st Avenue
Seattle, Washington 98121
(206) 441-1026

Owners Jeff Steichen and John Stafford opened the original Casa U-Betcha in Portland in 1986. Affectionately known as "Little Casa," it quickly became and still is the spot for great Mexican/New World food in an upbeat atmosphere.

In September 1989, the Seattle version was established although on a grander scale. Casa U-Betcha creates a high energy, lively atmosphere with its unusual decor. The large dining room is divided by zig-zagging half walls and is accented by turquoise, purple, screaming green, electric pink, blue and yellow. Faux lizard skin booths, an upside down pyramid, serpentine bar: a spirited gathering and dining place. Casa serves up creative neo-Mexican fare with flair.

Chef Lisa Esposito came to Casa U-Betcha two years ago from Denver, where she worked as sous-chef at "Cactus," specializing in Southwest and Southern cuisine. She incorporates a unique blend of flavors and foods from the Caribbean and Mediterranean into many of her specials which are on the menu daily. The recipes come from the soul, from the pure enjoyment of combining imagin-ation, fun and flavor to produce a satiated smile upon the lips of those who indulge.

Camarones Mazatlan

Serves 8

¼ c chili powder

¼ c paprika

¼ c black pepper

¼ c oregano

¼ c basil

¼ c sugar

3 Tbsp salt

¼ c fresh minced garlic

¼ c red wine vinegar

2 c olive oil

1 c vegetable oil

3 lbs med prawns, shell on, deveined

1 red bell pepper, fine dice

1 green bell pepper, fine dice

lemon for garnish

Combine all ingredients except for shrimp in a large work bowl. (This will keep in a covered jar in your refrigerator if you have any left over.)

Heat a large saute pan on medium heat. Add 1 cup of the oil mixture to the pan and lower heat. Add the prawns and peppers. Saute until prawns turn pink and remove from heat. Serve on rice or with flour tortillas. Garnish with lemon wedges and enjoy!

Cool Casa Gazpacho

Serves 6-8

2 cucumbers, peeled, seeded and
   small dice
1 red bell pepper, small dice
1 green bell pepper, small dice
½ sm red onion, fine dice
⅛ c minced fresh garlic
4 Tbsp olive oil
1 Tbsp Worcestershire sauce

4 c tomato juice
1 Tbsp salt
1 Tbsp black pepper
⅓ c sherry vinegar
⅓ c fresh lime juice
fresh cilantro sprigs and lime
   for garnish

Combine all ingredients and chill for at least four hours. Serve cold with cilantro and lime. This is a lovely and refreshing soup for summer, or anytime.

Soul Mama Caribbean Coconut-Lime Soup

Serves 8-10

3 Tbsp olive oil

2 Tbsp minced fresh ginger

2 med yellow onions, diced

2 lg green bell peppers, diced

2 lg red bell peppers, diced

1 jar Busha Browne's jerk
seasoning*

5 cans coconut milk

½ cup fresh lime juice

3 bunches fresh cilantro, chopped

½ cup fresh basil, chopped

1 tsp salt

¼ cup soy sauce

1 cup heavy cream

2 lbs sea scallops

2 lbs local mussels

2 lbs cockle clams

2 ea lemons and limes for garnish

In a large sauce pan, saute onions, peppers and ginger until onions are translucent. Add jerk seasoning and mix thoroughly.

Add remaining ingredients except for basil, cilantro and seafood. Bring to a boil.

Reduce heat and keep warm, adding the fresh basil and cilantro at this time.

Heat 1 tablespoon oil in a large saute pan. Add scallops, mussels and clams. Brown scallops on both sides. By this time clams and mussels should be opening up.

Add seafood to the soup and let simmer until mussels and clams have opened completely and are cooked.

Serve it up! Large flat bowls work beautifully so that the seafood shows amidst the soup and you can see all the delicious ingredients. Garnish with lemon and lime wheels twisted together.

*Available at specialty markets such as Larry's.

2726 East Cherry Street
(Corner of ML King Jr Way & E Cherry Street)
Seattle, Washington 98122
(206) 323-4330

Since 1985, a warm, friendly Southern hospitality is the atmosphere that greets you at this fast food restaurant where catfish which is "farm-raised" in large freshwater ponds is the specialty.

The catfish can be purchased whole, fillet, fillet bits or cajun style.

Other entrees include red snapper, buffalo fish and seafood gumbo. Dinners include an array of soul foods such as mustard greens, beans and rice, potato salad and a great coleslaw.

Catfish Corner's hamburgers, hot wings, prawns, melt-in-your-mouth hushpuppies and "Rosie's" homemade tartar sauce are huge successes.

"Auntie's" Famous Peach Cobbler is a must, and is a great late night snack.

Catfish Corner is open seven days a week. Food can be purchased to go or eaten in the homey, come-as-you-are restaurant. All of us at Catfish Corner are dedicated to making your visit memorable.

Try our catfish and if you like it, tell a friend, and if not, tell us! Our hours are: Monday to Friday 11:00am till 10:00pm; Saturday 12:00 noon till 10:00pm; Sunday 12:00 noon till 7:00pm.

Cornbread or Cornbread Muffins

Makes 1 loaf bread or 1 dozen muffins

1⅓ c all-purpose flour
⅔ c cornmeal
⅔ c sugar (optional)
½ c corn flour*
5 tsp baking powder

½ tsp salt
1⅓ c milk
5 Tbsp unsalted butter, melted
1 sm egg, beaten

In a large bowl, combine the flour, cornmeal, sugar, corn flour, baking powder and salt. Mix well, breaking up any lumps.

In a separate bowl combine the milk, butter and egg and add to dry ingredients. Blend just until mixed and large lumps are dissolved. Do not overbeat.

For bread: pour mixture into a greased 8"x8" baking pan and bake at 350° until golden brown, about 55 minutes. Remove from pan and serve immediately.

For muffins: spoon mixture into 12 greased muffin cups. Bake at 350° until golden brown, about 45 minutes. Remove from pan immediately and serve while hot.

Note: you can make your cornbread without sugar if you prefer. Cajuns like it sweet.

Hushpuppies

Makes about 30 hushpuppies

1 c cornmeal

½ c all-purpose flour

½ c corn flour*

1 Tbsp baking powder

¾ tsp ground red pepper
  (preferably cayenne)

½ tsp salt

½ tsp black pepper

½ tsp dried thyme leaves

¼ tsp white pepper

⅛ tsp dried oregano leaves

¼ c very finely chopped green
  olives (tops only)

1½ tsp minced garlic

2 eggs, beaten

1 c milk

2 Tbsp pork lard, unsalted butter,
  vegetable oil, chicken fat or
  bacon drippings

vegetable oil for deep frying

Combine all the dry ingredients in a large bowl, breaking up any lumps. Stir in the green onions and garlic. Add the eggs and blend well.

In a small saucepan, bring the milk and lard (or other fat) to a boil. Remove from heat and add to the flour mixture, half at a time, stirring well after each addition.

Refrigerate for 1 hour.

In a large skillet or deep fryer, heat 4 inches of oil to 350°. Drop the batter by tablespoonfuls into the hot oil. Do not crowd.

Cook until dark golden brown and cooked through, about 2 minutes. Drain on paper towels.

Note: corn flour is available at health food stores.

CHANDLER'S CRABHOUSE
AND FRESH FISH MARKET

901 Fairview Ave North
Seattle, Washington 98109
(206) 223-CRAB

Located on the south end of Lake Union, Chandler's Crabhouse serves "Seattle's Best Seafood." Chef Brian Poor offers a variety of crabs, shellfish and the finest selection of fresh fish in the Northwest. Retail sales available at the Fresh Fish Market.

Whiskied Crab Soup

Serves 6 to 8

1 Dungeness crab in shell,
  2 to 2½ lbs
4 oz butter (1 stick)
¾ c flour
1 qt crab stock (see recipe)
3 c heavy cream
¼ lemon
dash Tabasco

1 Tbsp Worcestershire
¼ tsp Old Bay seasoning*
¼ tsp ground white pepper
2 tsp whiskey
1 Tbsp dry sherry
2 Tbsp butter
salt to taste

Clean the crab and remove the meat from the shell. Reserve the meat. Use shell to make the crab stock.

Make a roux in a heavy sauce pan by melting 4 oz butter over medium heat. When the foam subsides, add the flour all at once. Stir constantly, reduce the heat to low, and cook, stirring until it is blond-colored, about 5 minutes.

Add crab stock, cup by cup, whisking thoroughly after each addition. Bring to boil, reduce to a simmer for 20 minutes, skimming frequently.

Add the heavy cream, juice from the lemon, Tabasco, Worcestershire, Old Bay, and white pepper and bring back to simmer for 10 minutes.

Add the whiskey, sherry, the 2 Tbsp butter, and the reserved crab meat. Cook 1 minute to heat through. Salt to taste.

Note: Old Bay seasoning is available for purchase in our Fish Market.

Crab Stock

Makes 1 quart

shells from 1 Dungeness crab
2 Tbsp olive oil
¼ c carrot, peeled and chopped
½ c onion, peeled and chopped
¼ c celery, chopped
¼ c brandy or cognac

1 qt cold water
2 cloves garlic, crushed, skin on
1 bay leaf
1 tsp dried tarragon
4 Tbsp tomato paste

Heat the olive oil in a heavy stock pot. Add the crab shells, carrots, onions, celery and brown lightly.

Add brandy and ignite. When flames have expired, add water, garlic, bay leaf, tarragon and tomato paste.

Bring stock to a low simmer for 2 to 3 hours, removing occasionally any scum which rises to the surface.

Strain through a fine sieve and refrigerate until ready to use.

Chandler's Crabhouse Crab Cakes

Makes 10 (2-2½ oz) patties

40 oz Dungeness crab, squeezed
  dry

2 oz white onion, minced

2 oz celery, minced

1 oz red bell pepper, minced

1 oz green bell pepper, minced

1 oz gold bell pepper, minced

1 Tbsp garlic, minced

3 med eggs

2½ Tbsp Best Foods mayonnaise

2½ Tbsp Worcestershire

2½ Tbsp fresh parsley, minced

2½ tsp Old Bay Seasoning*

3½ slices white bread, torn

1½ oz clarified butter

Crab should be well drained. Lightly saute vegetables. Whip eggs and add all spices. Mix crab, vegetables, egg mixture and bread well.

Shape into 2½ oz patties. Pan fry in clarified butter on medium-high heat until golden brown.

*Old Bay Seasoning is available for purchase in our Fish Market.

42

Key Lime Pie

Serves 4 – 6

Graham cracker crust:
1 c graham cracker crumbs
¼ c sugar
¼ c melted butter (½ stick)

Filling:
6 egg yolks
1½ 14-oz cans (21 oz) sweetened condensed milk
3¾ c Nellie & Joe's Key Lime Juice*
¾ c whipping cream
¼ c powdered sugar
⅛ tsp vanilla

Preheat oven to 350°. Whip the egg yolks until pale and nearly doubled in bulk. Whisk in the condensed milk, then the lime juice.

Fill the chilled shell and bake at 350° for 10 to 15 minutes, until golden brown. Remove and cool.

Whip the cream until stiff, adding sugar halfway through. Top pie. Serve immediately or refrigerate.

15600 NE 8th
Crossroads Shopping Center
Bellevue, Washington 98008
(206) 641-0500

Chili's Grill and Bar is a full service restaurant and lounge featuring a full array of appetizers, entrees and cocktails with a Southwestern, or "Tex-Mex" influence.

Specialties include fajitas, ribs, country fried steak or chicken, a variety of ½ pound burgers, salads and tacos. And – of course – chili!

Chili's is famous for its frosty top shelf and regular margaritas, but is equally well-known for unlimited refills on most non-alcoholic drinks.

Chili's serves its guests in a casual, up-beat environment with an emphasis on quality food and beverages. Kid's menu available.

Awesome Blossom

Serves 2

flour

paprika

colossal onion (19 oz or bigger)

your favorite deep-fry batter

"Blossom" sauce for dipping

Cut ends off of colossal onion, make 13 cuts ¼" apart to the edge of the core. Drop on cutting board to fan out.

Drip the fanned onion in batter mix. Flour the onion, making sure you evenly coat the entire onion, inside and out.

Deep fry the onion for 45 seconds on both sides. Decorate the heart of the onion, use blossom sauce for dipping!
"Bloom Sauce" is available at Chiles.

Chicken Quesadilla

Serves 2

4 6" flour tortillas (soft)

2 c Monterey Jack cheese

2 c cooked, shredded chicken breast

1 c pico de gallo made of diced tomatoes, onion and jalapeno peppers, or fresh salsa

sour cream for garnish

Place Jack cheese, chicken breast, and pico de gallo in between two 6" flour tortillas.

Place tortillas on flat grill (375°) and cook for 4 minutes, flip over and cook for 3 more minutes.

Cut cooked tortilla into 4 pieces. Place quarters of quesadilla on platter, garnish with sour cream and pico de gallo.

Crystal Mountain Resort

Summit House Mountain Top Restaurant
1 Crystal Mountain, Washington 98022
(206) 663-2265

Enjoy a sunset dinner at an elevation of almost 7,000 feet, the highest restaurant in the state! The menu features delicious Northwest cuisine, tantalizing nightly specials, an impressive wine list, and a wide variety of beers. Sunset dinners are served Friday, Saturday and Sunday evenings from 5:00 to 8:00pm. Advance reservations are required, and can be made by calling (206) 663-2300.

Situated in the Mount Baker-Snoqualmie National Forest, Crystal Mountain is 64 miles from Tacoma, 76 miles from Seattle, and 80 miles from Yakima.

Chicken Florentine

Serves 12

1 pkg frozen puff pastry, thawed, but chilled

12 8-oz chicken breasts, boneless, skinless

fresh spinach

2 pints whipping cream

thyme

basil

garlic

4-6 eggs

¼ lb flour

¼ lb butter

Make up roux by combining ¼ lb flour and ¼ lb butter over low flame. Heat 2 pints of whipping cream until simmering. Add roux to whipping cream until whip marks show. Let cool.

Add dashes of salt, garlic, thyme, and basil. Wash, stem and coarsely chop ½ lb spinach. Add spinach to cream and mix well.

Cut puff pastry sheets into thirds, to make 12 rectangles. Place 8 oz boneless, skinless chicken breast in what would be skin side down on a rectangle of pastry.

Add 3 oz ladle full of spinach/cream mixture on top of chicken. Wrap puff pastry around chicken and seal edges with floured fork.

Crack 4 eggs and beat until broken. Then egg-wash entire top of pastry.

Bake at 400 degrees for 20 minutes, pastry shell should be golden brown.

Seafood en Papilotte

Serves 4

2 lbs halibut, steak or fillet
1 lb shrimp (15 count)
½ lb butter
shallots

1 lg red pepper
1 lemon
parchment paper

Cut halibut into 8 oz portions. Peel shrimp. Slice a lemon into ¼" thick wheels.

Prepare red pepper shallot butter as follows: peel red pepper by blackening over flame, peeling black layer off. Then dice. Add ½ lb butter and 1 Tbsp minced shallots into bowl. Mix until smooth.

Spread red pepper shallot butter in oval pattern in center of parchment paper. Place halibut at base of oval spread. Place lemon wheel on top of halibut. Place shrimp on top of lemon wheel. Fold over top of parchment paper, then tightly roll loose ends toward halibut.

Cook at 400 degrees for 15 minutes.

CUCINA! CUCINA!®
ITALIAN · CAFE

901 Fairview Ave North
Seattle, Washington 98109
44-PASTA

In a fun, upbeat atmosphere, chef Mikel Rogers serves a variety of "cutting edge" as well as traditional Italian favorites, featuring pizzas from our woodburning ovens and a vast selection of appetizers, pastas, salads and desserts. Children and their birthday celebrations are always welcome at Cucina Cucina.

Sausage/Lentil Soup

Serves 10

1¼ c dry lentils

10 oz bulk Italian sausage, cooked

1 oz whole butter

1½ oz white onions, diced ¼"

1½ oz carrots, diced ¼"

4 oz leeks, white part only, diced ½"

6 oz celery, ¼" diced

3 c chicken stock, fresh or canned

¾ oz Dijon mustard

1 Tbsp red wine vinegar

6½ oz heavy cream

1 tsp salt

⅛ tsp ground white pepper

1½ oz chiffonade spinach, washed and sliced ½"

Rinse lentils, cover with 1" water and soak overnight. Drain and rinse again.

Saute sausage, butter and vegetables in a large pot until light brown. Add chicken stock and lentils, bring to a boil, reduce to a simmer and cook 40 minutes.

Add mustard, vinegar, cream, salt and white pepper and cook 10 minutes. Adjust seasonings. Add spinach, cook 5 minutes.

Place hot soup in appropriate dishes (soup cup or bowl).

Float 1 Tbsp tomato sauce in the center of each bowl. Sprinkle parmesan across tomato sauce.

Pasta with Tomato, Garlic, Basil Sauce

Serves 4-6

1 c olive oil

4 oz sliced elephant garlic

4 oz minced garlic

4 oz basil, chiffonade

3½ c diced Roma tomatoes

4 tsp kosher salt

¼ tsp crushed red peppers

1½ c chicken stock, fresh or canned

1 c tomato sauce

1 lb angel hair paste

½ c olive oil

4 oz grated parmesan cheese

½ oz chiffonade basil

Heat olive oil with garlic until garlic is translucent. Add tomatoes and seasonings. Add chicken stock and tomato sauce, simmer.

Cook pasta to al dente (this thin pasta cooks very quickly). Drain.

Toss the pasta with the olive oil and sauce. Place on plate and serve with parmesan and basil.

Cucina! Cucina! Chopped Salad

Serves 8

4 oz cooked chicken peas, lightly chopped

1½ lb Iceberg lettuce, chopped ¼" to ½"

½ oz fresh basil, chopped

4 oz coarsely grated mozzarella cheese

12 oz diced poached breast of chicken

8 oz dry wine salami, diced

8 oz diced Roma Tomatoes, reserve half for garnish

2 oz grated Provolone cheese, reserve half for garnish

1 oz chopped scallions, reserve half for garnish

eight attractive lettuce leaves

Toss all ingredients in mixing bowl with 1½ cups Italian Vinaigrette. Divide evenly on plates lined with lettuce leaves. Garnish with remaining tomatoes, provolone and scallions.

Cucina! Cucina! Italian Vinaigrette

Makes 1½ cups

1 egg yolk
1 Tbsp Dijon mustard
2 Tbsp minced fresh garlic
½ tsp Kosher salt
1 tsp coarse black pepper
½ tsp dry mustard

2 tsp dried oregano
½ tsp sugar
3 oz red wine vinegar
1 c virgin olive oil
2 Tbsp fresh lemon juice

Combine yolk, garlic, salt, pepper, Dijon mustard, dry mustard, oregano, and sugar in mixing bowl. Whisk well. Add vinegar and whisk again. Add olive oil in a stream, whisking finish with lemon juice.

635 Elliott Avenue West
Seattle, Washington 98119
(206) 286-6842

Darigold ensures the highest standard of quality because our products are made locally with the freshest of ingredients.

Darigold, Inc. is the marketing arm of Darigold Farms, a dairy cooperative representing approximately 1400 dairy farmers from Washington, Oregon, Idaho and Northern California. Its headquarters are located in Seattle, Washington.

The Darigold cooperative organization was formed in 1918, and is the 8th largest regional dairy cooperative in the United States.

Honey Dew Meringues

Serves 4

1 8-oz carton Darigold Raspberry
   Lowfat Yogurt
4 c cantaloupe, cut in chunks
4 c berries (any combination of
   blackberries, raspberries,
   strawberries or blueberries)

2 honeydew melons
4 egg whites, or Crescent
   Meringue mix
1 tsp vanilla
½ tsp cream of tartar
½ c sugar

Combine yogurt, cantaloupe and berries. Cut honeydew melons in half, scoop out pulp and fill with berry mixture.

Beat egg whites with vanilla and cream of tartar until frothy. Gradually beat in sugar, a little at a time. Beat until all sugar is dissolved and meringue is stiff and glossy. Spread on top of filling and rim of melon. Bake in a 475 degree oven 5 or 6 minutes or until meringue is golden.

Note: Serve with muffins, croissants or scones to make a complete meal. Granola may be folded into fruit mixture as part of filling.

Darigold's Classic Red Boy Chowder

Serves 6-8

4 slices bacon, chopped
1½ c onion, chopped
3 c potatoes, peeled and cubed
2 c water
2 Knorr Fish Flavor Bouillon
  cubes
1 tsp thyme
1 bay leaf
¼ tsp pepper

salt to taste
2 Tbsp Darigold butter
2 Tbsp flour
1 pint (2 cups) Darigold Classic
  Whipping Cream
1 tsp minced garlic
4 oz Darigold Red Boy Cheddar
  Cheese, shredded
8 oz minced clams

In a heavy 4-quart pan fry bacon until crisp; add onions and cook until tender. Add potatoes, water, bouillon cubes and seasonings. Cover and cook for 15 minutes or until potatoes are tender.

In a separate saucepan on low heat melt butter. Whisk in flour and cook 5 minutes or until blonde in color.

Add butter-flour mixture and whipping cream to soup base. Cook on medium heat 5 minutes or until thickened. Stir in garlic, cheese and clams. Heat thoroughly but do not boil.

Cheesy Fondue Gratin

Serves 4

2 Tbsp Darigold butter

2 Tbsp olive oil

1 sm loaf French bread, cut into cubes (about 5 cups)

3 c Darigold 2% milk

2 Tbsp flour

¼ tsp thyme

½ tsp oregano

½ tsp garlic powder

¼ tsp cayenne

¼ tsp dried mustard

1 tsp Worcestershire sauce

salt and pepper to taste

3 c Darigold Swiss cheese, shredded

Melt butter and mix in olive oil. Spread bread cubes on a baking sheet and drizzle with the butter/olive oil mixture. Bake bread cubes in a 350 degree oven 20 to 30 minutes, stirring occasionally until crisp and tasty. Transfer bread cubes to a 1½ quart ovenproof baking dish.

Meanwhile, place shredded cheese in a large mixing bowl, set aside. In a medium saucepan, combine *cold* milk, flour, Worcestershire sauce and herbs, mixing with a wire whisk until smooth. Heat milk mixture just to boiling. Stir hot milk mixture into shredded cheese, mixing well, and pour over bread. Bake at 400 degrees until hot and bubbly, 5 to 10 minutes. Serve immediately.

For tasty variations try: (1) Darigold Monterey Pepper Jack Cheese (omitting Worcestershire sauce) instead of Darigold Swiss Cheese, ¼ c chopped green onions and ½ lb ground beef, cooked, drained and crumbled, sprinkled on top; (2) One half pound crab meat, coarsely chopped, and sliced almonds sprinkled on top; (3) One half pound Italian sausage, cooked, drained and crumbled, 3 Tbsp chopped parsley and 3 Tbsp shredded Parmesan cheese sprinkled on top; (4) Sprinkle 8 strips bacon that has been cooked, drained and crumbled, plus 5 chopped green onions over the top.

15600 NE 8th Street
Bellevue, Washington 98008
(206) 641-4352

About our name: EBRU is a traditional Turkish art. Little is known about the origins of the art of EBRU or marbling. The oldest known example of EBRU, whose practitioners today are precious and few, dates back to 1554.

The term itself comes from the Persian word meaning eyebrow and cloud. One type of EBRU is known as "battal" (or plain). EBRU consists of forms reminiscent of eyebrow and cloud shapes. The materials used in making EBRU are dye (all earthen), kitre (gum tragacanth), od (bile), tekre (trough), firca (brush), combs, wire, paper (almost any kind) and muhre (polishing stone).

EBRU in light colors is used as a background for calligraphy, bookbinding and other forms of art.

In the Mediterranean, names give meaning to the establishment in which they are named. We believe our service and food are quality – just as the Turkish art of EBRU.

We are open seven days a week for breakfast, lunch, dinner, and take home. Enjoy our new early 7:00 am opening and Friday–Saturday late night 10:30 pm closing with entertainment (free). Come and enjoy our many kinds of baklava, fresh hand-squeezed juices, hot gyro sandwiches, filled pastries, many mouth-watering Mediterranean salads, grocery items and smiling faces to serve you.

Turkish Coffee

Serves 5

1½ c cold water   6 tsp Turkish coffee (pulverized)

3 - 6 tsp sugar   optional: ⅛ tsp ground cardamom

In a special brass coffee pot, bring water and sugar to a boil. Add coffee (and cardamom, if desired), and stir well.

Bring to a boil until foam rises to top of pot. Remove from heat and let the foam subside.

Bring to a boil again, remove from heat, and let foam subside two more times.

After coffee has foamed and subsided three times, pour it immediately into demitasse cups. Allow grinds to settle in cups a minute or two before drinking. Drink very hot.

Marinated Eggplant Salad

Serves 6

1 lg eggplant
2 med tomatoes, quartered
½ sm onion, finely diced
2 Tbsp chopped parsley
½ c olive oil

⅓ c lemon juice or vinegar
1 tsp salt
¼ tsp pepper
2 cloves garlic, crushed

Bake eggplant at 350 degrees for thirty minutes. Dip in cold water immediately and peel. Dice and place in salad bowl.

Mix eggplant, tomatoes, onions, parsley, oil, lemon and seasonings. Marinate 1 hour. Serve at room temperature.

GLOBAL VILLAGE
COOKING SCHOOL

P.O. Box 51115
Seattle, Washington 98115
(206) 464-0160

Global Village is not a cooking school in the traditional sense. While we do offer classes in Seattle and on our cooking tour to Bangkok, most of our classes are "correspondence courses" – culinary adventures available by mail.

Global Village makes it easy for the adventurous cook to make authentic international meals at home. We track down hard-to-find ingredients from around the world, explain what they are and how to use them, then package them together with authentic recipes, cultural information, maps and postcards. Our self-contained kits bring the world to your doorstep. You don't even have to renew your passport.

For example, our Thai baskets overflow with spices, sauces and pastas imported from Thailand. We also include a booklet with clear, easy recipes, explanations of ingredients, and information on Thai culture and food in Thailand.

Come with us on our culinary adventure. This time, the trip's on us.

Thai-Style Noodles (Pad Thai)

Serves 2

1 1-lb pkg rice stick noodles

1 Tbsp vegetable or peanut oil

2 cloves garlic, minced, or

1 Tbsp chili-garlic paste

1 tsp tomato paste

¼ c rice vinegar

2 Tbsp sugar

2 Tbsp fish sauce, or to taste

8 lg shrimp, shelled and deveined

1 egg, beaten

1 c fresh bean sprouts

1 c green onion, cut into 1" pieces

Cilantro, lime wedges, and roasted salted peanuts (chopped) for garnish

Soak half the package of noodles in lukewarm water to soften. Check the noodles every five minutes. The consistency of the noodles is the secret of this dish. Noodles should be soft enough to fry, but with a slightly rubbery consistency. Every brand of noodles will need to soak for a different amount of time. Never let them get as soft as cooked pasta. Drain noodles and set aside. In a small bowl, combine tomato paste, rice vinegar and sugar. If you are using a chili-garlic paste instead of plain garlic (which will make this dish spicy) you may omit the tomato paste. Set aside.

Heat wok or frypan and add oil. Saute garlic or chili-garlic paste until fragrant; add shrimp. Sprinkle with a little fish sauce. When shrimp are cooked, add half of the vinegar mixture and stir well. Add noodles, mix well until thoroughly coated. If noodles seem too dry, add the rest of the vinegar mixture. Push the noodles to one side and pour in the egg. Stir until soft scrambled, and mix well with the noodles. Continue to cook for another minute, adding another teaspoon of fish sauce.

Mix in half the bean sprouts and half the green onions. Stir well and remove from heat. Garnish with remaining bean sprouts, green onions, cilantro, peanuts and lime wedges.

Shrimp in Spicy Chili Oil
Koong Phat Nam Prik Pao

Serves 2

1 Tbsp vegetable or peanut oil

3 cloves garlic, minced

½ lb shrimp, shelled and deveined

2 Tbsp fish sauce, or to taste

2 Tbsp roasted chili paste in oil*

1 Tbsp sugar

cilantro for garnish

Heat wok or frypan until hot. Add oil. When oil is hot, saute garlic until slightly golden. Immediately add shrimp and sprinkle with 1 Tbsp of the fish sauce.

Continue to stir fry until shrimp are just cooked through. Add the roasted chili paste and stir until evenly mixed. Allow to bubble vigorously for one minute. Add the remaining fish sauce and the sugar. Stir well and remove from heat. Garnish with cilantro.

*Called "nam prik pao" in Thai, this thick paste of roasted shrimp, chilies, garlic, tamarind and onion is rich brown in color and comes in glass jars. Sometimes called "roasted chili in oil."

*Special ingredients are available at Viet Wah Supermarket on Jackson Street, Welcome Supermarket on 12th & Jackson, and any other Asian store carrying ingredients from Southeast Asia.

C A F F E   I T A L I A N O

2301 N. 30th
Tacoma, Washington
(206) 627-0231
CAFFE ITALIANO
16943 Southcenter Parkway
Tukwila, Washington
(206) 575-1606
RISTORANTE & CATERING
3820 124th SE
Bellevue, Washington
(206) 644-1200
Catering: (206) 726-6298

In a turn-of-the-century building overlooking the bay in Tacoma, Grazie features Northern Italian cuisine presented in a warm, comfortable atmosphere. Menu selections include espresso, antipasto, fresh seafoods, pasta, veal and desserts. Grazie also has a full-service Italian deli, outdoor seating and lounge.

Grazie Cafe, located three blocks from Southcenter Mall, features our antipasti, poultry, pastas and desserts, all served from an entertaining exhibition kitchen. Come and try our new Bellevue Ristorante and enjoy the foods that have made us popular.

Catering and banquet facilities are available in Tacoma and Bellevue.

Farfalle con Pollo di Grigillia

Serves 1

3½ oz chicken breast, boneless,
  lightly pounded
1 oz olive oil
6 oz Farfalle (bow-tie pasta)
6 calamata olives, halved
6 Roma tomato slices
½ tsp garlic, minced

½ tsp basil
¼ tsp oregano
1 oz white wine
2 oz chicken stock
2 oz tomato sauce
1 Tbsp hard butter
1 oz Asiago cheese

Heat a saute pan over medium high flame, add olive oil, garlic, basil, oregano and calamata olives, flame with white wine.

Add chicken stock, tomato sauce, and Roma tomato slices. Reduce to proper consistency.

Cook pasta and drain. Add pasta and butter. Toss to coat pasta thoroughly. Place pasta in a bowl, top with Asiago cheese.

Season chicken with seasoned salt. Broil until just done. Remove chicken, cut into 5 pieces, place in a fan on top of pasta, garnish with fresh parsley and serve.

Scallopine al Noce e Jettisimo

Serves 1

1 4-oz veal scallop
¼ c mushrooms. sliced
1½ oz olive oil
1 oz sherry
2 oz veal stock
1½ oz cream
½ tsp garlic, pureed

¼ tsp paprika
parsley, chopped
seasoning salt to taste
Pistachio/bread crumb mix:
2 c bread crumbs
1 c pistachios, ground
¼ c parsley, chopped

To make pistachio/bread crumb mix, combine all ingredients.

Heat a steel pan with olive oil, add veal and saute, season both sides.

Remove veal and allow grease to drain. Add mushrooms and garlic, saute until golden, flame with sherry, add paprika, parsley, stock and cream. Reduce to proper consistency.

Remove mushroom slices and place them halfway under the scallops of veal. Pour sauce over the top.

Hiram's
At The Locks

5300 34th NW
Seattle, Washington 98107
(206) 784-1733

For over 10 years, Hiram's has given Seattle the kind of casual elegance in dining that makes for a great meal. The restaurant specializes in a variety of fresh Northwest seafoods and features the same dry cured, 28-day aged beef as the Metropolitan Grill.

Hiram's, named after Hiram Chittenden, designer of the locks at Shilshole Bay, has a sweeping view of the water and boat traffic, providing entertainment any time of the day. During nice weather, Hiram's large patio overlooking the water is open for lunch, dinner, Sunday brunch or for cocktails and appetizers.

With the spectacular backdrop of the water, the variety and quality of the menu and the enticement of the patio, Hiram's has established itself as one of Seattle's landmark restaurants.

Roast Tenderloin Filet
with Port Wine & Wild Mushroom Sauce

Serves 4

4 ea 12- to 14-oz tenderloin filets
steak seasoning
16 toasted long French bread
   croutons
⅛ c pure olive oil

1 lb chantrelle, shitake, or morel
   mushrooms
1 c port wine
1 Tbsp minced fresh shallots
1 c (rich) demi glace or brown
   sauce
2 Tbsp unsalted butter

Heat oven to 400 degrees. In large ovenproof skillet, heat oil till bubbling. Season filets fairly evenly and place in skillet, turning on all sides and ends till nicely brown. Place in oven for approximately 12 to 14 minutes for medium rare, a few minutes longer for medium to medium well. Turn meat over at 6 to 7 minutes.

Meanwhile, wash mushrooms, pat dry and quarter. In sauce pan, heat unsalted butter till melted. Saute shallots and mushrooms, season with salt and pepper to taste, add ¾ c port wine and reduce by two thirds. Add demi glace or brown sauce and simmer till steaks are done. Remove steaks, discard oil from skillet, and add remaining port wine to remove pan drippings. Add to mushroom sauce and adjust seasonings to taste.

Fan croutons on plates and slice each steak 3 to 4 cuts each. Lay over croutons and top with port wine sauce.

Crab Dip

Serves 4

4 oz crab meat
8 oz artichoke hearts
3 oz cream
½ oz roux*
1 oz Rondele cheese

½ cup celery, onion & mushroom mix
1 squirt Worcestershire sauce
1 pinch steak seasoning
1 tsp Dijon mustard
2 oz mayonnaise

Drain crab meat and artichoke hearts very, very, very well. Boil the cream, roux and Rondele cheese and cool. Saute celery, onion and mushroom mix. Mix all ingredients together and check seasoning. Serve with French bread, crackers or tortilla chips.

*Roux – a thickening paste made of butter and flour.

Mesquite Broiled Salmon with Pesto

Serves 2

2 8-oz salmon fillets
½ cup olive oil
½ cup salad oil
¼ cup minced garlic

⅓ cup chopped basil
⅓ cup roasted pine nuts
zest of one lemon
salt to taste

In a medium size bowl, add all ingredients together except salmon fillets and pine nuts. Let stand one hour.

Trim salmon fillets to remove any bones or skin which may be present. Chop pine nuts and add to pesto marinade, mix well. Add salmon fillets and let marinate 6 hours under refrigeration, turning salmon fillets over every two hours.

Remove from marinade and grill over mesquite charcoal 3 to 4 minutes on each side. Remove from grill and brush on pesto marinade to taste.

Enjoy!

HIRAM WALKER

& SONS, INC.

KAHLÚA COMEDY CLUB

Kahlua Coffee

Serves 1

1½ oz Kahlua
chilled coffee
cream or milk, if desired

Pour Kahlua over coffee in mug. Add cream or milk, if you like. Stir.

Kahlua & Soda

Serves 1

1½ oz Kahlua
club soda
lime wedge

Pour Kahlua over ice in a highball glass. Add club soda. Stir. Garnish with lime wedge, if desired.

Kahlua White Russian

Serves 1

1 oz Kahlua
1 oz vodka
2 oz cream or milk

Pour Kahlua and vodka over ice. Top with fresh cream or milk. Stir.

Kahlua Black Russian

Serves 1

1 oz Kahlua
1½ oz vodka

Pour Kahlua and vodka over ice in an old-fashioned glass. Stir.

Kahlua Hummer

Serves 1

1 oz Kahlua
1 oz light rum
2 scoops French vanilla or
   chocolate ice cream

Combine and blend briefly. To make by the pitcher: use 6 oz Kahlua, 6 oz light rum and 20 oz (2½ cups) ice cream.

Kahlua Pola Bear

Serves 1

1 oz Kahlua
1 oz vodka
2 scoops vanilla ice cream

Combine and blend briefly.

HYATT REGENCY ✪ BELLEVUE

At Bellevue Plaza Place
900 Bellevue Way
Bellevue, Washington 98004
(206) 462-1234

Spectacular views of the Seattle skyline, majestic Mt Rainier and beautiful Lake Washington compliment the comfort and luxuries offered by the Hyatt Regency Bellevue.

As a self contained world where choices never end, the Bellevue Place complex offers upscale boutiques, an array of cuisines, business services and first class athletic facilities all under one roof.

Bellevue Place, a place for people.

Smoked Chicken & Cheese Sandwich

with Seasoned Olive Oil

Serves 10

20 oz smoked chicken, sliced
10 oz cheddar cheese, sliced
1 ea focaccia bread

Seasoned olive oil:
6 oz olive oil
1 Tbsp chopped garlic
2 Tbsp sweet basil
salt & pepper to taste

Mix olive oil ingredients and let stand overnight.

Slice focaccia bread in half to form two sandwich halves. Brush seasoned olive oil on bread. Layer chicken and sliced cheese on bread. Top with the second half of bread. Grill until done.

Hot Italian Sandwich

Serves 10

1 ea focaccia bread

10 oz sliced prosciutto

10 oz sliced smoked ham

10 oz sliced provolone cheese

5 oz pesto sauce

2 oz seasoned olive oil
(see preceding recipe)

Prepare seasoned olive oil according to preceding recipe.

Slice focaccia bread in half to form two sandwich halves. Brush seasoned olive oil and then pesto sauce on bread. Layer prosciutto, ham and provolone cheese on bread. Top with second half of bread. Grill until done.

THE KALEENKA

A RUSSIAN RESTAURANT

1933 First Avenue at Virginia Street
Seattle, Washington
(206) 728-1278

The Kaleenka features the foods of the Russian people – strange and tasty dishes developed through the ages by the country folk. Many of these are regional, from the Ukraine, Georgia, and Uzbekestan, reflecting the tastes of these peoples and the fruits of the land. Americans take to these dishes readily and love them from the first bite.

All dishes and desserts are prepared in the Kaleenka kitchen, using ingredients and fresh produce from the Pike Place Market. Our chefs have been trained in America and by renowned Russian chefs, which is your assurance of authentic high quality fare.

The Kaleenka serves imported beer from Poland, Norway, Czechoslovakia, and wines from Georgia, Hungary, and Yugoslavia. Ethnic decor, friendly staff, authentic foods and a Slavic ambiance make for a memorable Russian evening.

Piroshky

Dough:
1½ pkgs dry yeast
¼ cup warm water
2 Tbsp sugar
1 tsp salt
1½ cups milk
1 egg
¼ cup oil or butter
4-5 cups flour

Filling:
1 med onion, chopped
2 lbs ground round beef
1 clove garlic, minced
salt
pepper

A pirozhok is singular for piroshky. Both words derive from the Russian word *pin*, which means feast. Piroshky are a miniature feast.

Dissolve yeast in water. Let stand 10 minutes.

In large bowl combine flour, sugar and salt. Make a well in flour and add milk, egg, oil and yeast. Combine to make a soft dough. Knead about 10 minutes. Let rise one half hour to one hour.

Brown chopped onion and garlic. In separate pan, brown ground beef. Season with salt, pepper, garlic and onion. Cool meat mixture and remove solidified fat.

Pinch a golf-ball sized piece of dough, flatten with fingers or roll out to ⅛" thickness. Place 2 Tbsp filling in center and bring opposite edges of circle together and pinch securely. (The traditional shape is a plump center with tapering edges.)

Let piroshky rise seam side down, 30 minutes.

Heat oven to 350°. Brush piroshky with egg yolk and bake till golden brown. They may also be deep fried.

Samsa

Filling:
1 lb ground lamb
2 med onions, chopped finely
2 Tbsp whole cumin
1½ tsp salt
½ tsp pepper

Dough:
2 eggs
2 cups water
4 to 6 cups flour
2 Tbsp butter
2 to 3 Tbsp poppy seeds

To prepare filling: mix lamb and onion together, add cumin, salt and pepper. Set aside.

For dough: in mixer, combine 1 egg, 2 cups water and 4 cups flour. Mix. The dough should be soft but not sticky – if it's sticky, add more flour; if too dry, add more water.

Remove dough from mixer and place on floured surface. Knead 4-5 times and cover. Let rest for 10 minutes.

Cut dough into quarters. Take one quarter and place on floured surface and roll out to ¼" thickness. Cut into rounds about 4" diameter.

In center of each dough circle place 1 tsp of filling. Pinch opposite sides together. Place on greased baking sheet, seam side down. Brush with egg wash (egg beaten with water) and sprinkle with poppy seeds. Bake at 350° for 25-30 minutes.

Borshch

Serves 4–6

1 med onion, chopped
1 to 3 carrots, grated
1 to 2 beets, grated
1 potato, cubed
2 cups coarsely cut cabbage
½ green pepper, chopped
½ stalk celery, chopped
1 clove garlic

1 cup tomato juice
3 Tbsp oil
3 to 4 cups water
salt
pepper
fresh or dried dill (garnish)
sour cream (garnish)

This is a traditional Ukranian soup, served at Lent without meat.

Brown onion, carrots, and beets separately in 1 Tbsp of oil each. Set aside.

In saucepan bring 3 to 4 cups water to boiling and add remaining vegetables. Bring back to boiling and add onions, carrots and beets. Cook till vegetables are tender.

Add salt and pepper to taste, and tomato juice.

Serve piping hot with 1 tsp chopped fresh dill and a dollop of sour cream in each bowl. Accompany soup with a good rye bread.

Karam's

Simply Irresistible Cuisine & A Garlic Lover's Paradise
340 15th Avenue East, Seattle, Washington 98112
(206) 324-2370

Our recipes are unique creations developed in our kitchen. We continue a tradition which cherishes quality and freshness of ingredients and the presentation of good food as a celebration of life.

Try our fresh char-broiled chicken with Karam's Garlic Sauce, which came in first place at the Bite of Seattle. Our juicy, succulent char-broiled stuffed Kibbeh was also a real hit (first place again). If you haven't eaten eggplant before or do not think you really like it, take the plunge and give Baba-Ghannouj a try. And Karamage, another new palate-pleasing experience, of fresh homemade goat's milk cream cheese with garlic, mint and oregano. A highly requested appetizer.

We have also taken great care in selecting wines and beers to complement our menu. Chateau Musar from Lebanon, Royal Moghreb from Morocco and Sidi Brahim from Algeria. Beers include Rauchbier (smoked beer) from Bavaria, Germany, Lindemans Kriek, a cherry beer from Belgium, and a great local beer, Pike Place Ale, from Pike Place Brewery at the Public Market. Come experience and enjoy a touch of garlic paradise.

Karam's Garlic Sauce, Tahini Garlic Sauce, Baba Ghannouj and Hummus can be purchased at all Larry's Markets, Rainbow Grocery and QFC on 15th Avenue East and The Central Co-op on 12th Avenue East.

Salatit Hummus Maslouq
Garbanzo Bean Salad

Serves 2-3

2½ c garbanzo beans
water
½ tsp baking soda

sumac (optional)
Karam's Garlic Sauce

Soak beans overnight in 4 quarts cold water with ½ teaspoon soda. Rinse thoroughly, picking out any discolored beans. Boil gently in just enough water to cover beans during cooking.

Cook beans until very tender (beans can be easily mashed between fingers), approximately 3 hours.

Drain beans. Toss well with Karam's Garlic Sauce. Serve warm or cold. Enjoy!

Zahra (Fried Cauliflower)

Serves 3-4

1 med cauliflower
oil for deep frying

Karam's Tahini Garlic Sauce
sumac (optional)

Break cauliflower into florets and place in a bowl of lightly salted water. Soak for 15 minutes. Rinse and drain well.

Deep fry in a wok or deep fryer. Cook until golden brown. Remove from oil and drain on a paper towel.

Serve over romaine or rice. Drench with Karam's Tahini Garlic Sauce and sprinkle with sumac. Serve immediately. Enjoy!

LIAISON

401 Lenora
Seattle, Washington 98121
(206) 443-4300

The Liaison Restaurant is located downtown on 4th & Lenora, and features only the finest of foods prepared with the freshest seasonal Northwest ingredients. Live piano entertainment Monday – Saturday with New Jazz sessions on Friday and Saturdays nights from 9:30 pm to 1 am. No cover charge.

Chocolate Grand Marnier Mousse

Serves 10

¾ lb chocolate, semi-sweet

½ cup espresso

2 egg yolks

4 egg whites

1 pint whipping cream

½ cup sugar

¼ cup Grand Marnier

1 tsp vanilla

In a large mixing bowl, melt chocolate over steaming water. Keep warm. In a separate bowl, whip the cream with sugar until medium peaks form. Return to the chocolate and add the espresso, Grand Marnier, and vanilla. Then beat in the egg yolks one at a time. Mixture should stiffen. Then beat in one third of the whipped cream and fold in the rest. Again in a separate mixing bowl, whip the egg whites to stiff peaks, then fold them into the chocolate mixture and refrigerate until firm, 2 to 4 hours. Pipe into wine or champagne glasses with pastry bag and star tip.

Smoked Chicken Fettuccine

with Rosemary & Brandy

Serves 2

6 oz smoked chicken
4 oz bacon
10 oz fettuccine, cooked
1 tsp fresh rosemary
1 tsp garlic
1 tsp shallots
8 oz vin blanc (white wine)

8 oz cream
salt and pepper to taste
3 oz brandy
1 oz Parmesan cheese
red pepper
1 Tbsp olive oil

Cut smoked chicken into bite size pieces. Repeat with bacon. Peel and chop shallots and garlic. Clean and chop fresh rosemary. Julienne the red pepper.

Make Vin Blanc cream sauce: heat a 12" skillet, then add olive oil and allow to coat the bottom. Add chopped bacon and allow to saute for 2-3 minutes. Add chopped garlic, shallots, rosemary and smoked chicken. Toss occasionally for the next two minutes.

Deglaze the pan by adding brandy and allowing the alcohol to cook out. Add vin blanc and cream. Reduce to desired consistency.

Add fettuccine and heat. Add salt and pepper to taste. Garnish with grated Parmesan cheese and julienned red pepper.

Vin Blanc Cream Sauce

Makes six 4-oz servings

½ med white onion	4 cups white wine
1 med leek	4 cups fish stock
6 med mushrooms	4 cups heavy cream
¼ cup parsley	1 Tbsp olive oil

Chop and rinse all vegetables. In an eight-cup saucepan, heat the olive oil and saute vegetables until onion becomes clear. Add the white wine and reduce until the liquid is nearly gone. Then add the fish stock and reduce once again until the liquid is nearly gone.

Add the cream and bring to a boil. Reduce heat and simmer for about ten minutes. Be sure to stir occasionally as the pot boils to prevent sticking or burning. Remove from heat and strain sauce through a cheesecloth.

MARTINELLI'S SPARKING CIDER

S. Martinelli & Company
P.O. Box 1868
Watsonville, CA 95077

Produced in the same Watsonville, California location since 1868, Martinelli's Gold Medal Sparkling Cider and Apple Juice are made from only U.S. grown, fresh apples and contain absolutely no concentrates, no added water, no preservatives, no sweeteners and no additives of any kind. Winner of more than 50 gold medal awards, Martinelli's is available throughout the U.S. and in several foreign countries.

Acapulco Sunset

Serves 2

1 cup sliced fresh strawberries

½ c chopped seeded papaya

1 oz lime juice

1½ Tbsp sugar

10 oz Martinelli's Sparkling Cider

In blender combine sliced strawberries, papaya, lime juice, sugar, and Sparkling Cider. Whirl until smooth and well blended. Pour over crushed ice in two 10 to 12 oz glasses; garnish rim of each with a whole strawberry. Serve with straws. Makes 2 drinks.

Martinelli's Roast Chicken

1 3- to 3½-lb chicken	1¼ c Martinelli's Cider
4 lg carrots	1 bay leaf
2 med onions, peeled and	½ lemon
quartered	1 apple, cut into wedges
2 lg cloves garlic, quartered	salt, pepper, dried thyme

Preheat oven to 450 degrees. Remove giblets from chicken and remove the loose flap of fat at back of bird and set aside.

Peel carrots and cut into 2-inch chunks. In a shallow, non-reactive (enamel or glass) pan that's not much wider than bird, make a bed of carrots, onions, apples and one of the garlic cloves. Pour in Cider to coat.

Rinse the chicken and pat dry. Put chicken on bed and stuff with other clove of garlic, bay leaf and lemon. Place the reserved flap of fat at the apex of the breast so that it will baste. Leave legs loose, do not truss. Sprinkle bird with salt and pepper and crumble a generous tablespoon of thyme over all. Put chicken in oven and turn heat down to 425 degrees.

Cook for about an hour; bird should be brown and skin crackly. Check to see that juices are clear in color, not pink. Prepare gravy from juices remaining after vegetables are removed, if desired. Serve with roasted vegetables on the side.

Chilled Martinelli's Sabayon

Serves 24

15 egg yolks
8 oz sugar
1 c white wine
2 c Martinelli's Cider

4 oz frozen apple juice concentrate
1 qt whipping cream, whipped
8 sheets gelatin

Warm in a double boiler over simmering, not boiling, water: yolks, sugar, wine, Cider and juice concentrate. Once warmed, transfer to a bowl and beat with an electric mixer until cold.

Soften gelatin sheets in cold water. Remove from water and melt in saucepan over low heat. Add to Cider mixture. Fold in whipped cream. Pipe into champagne glasses. Serves 24.
Recipe courtesy of Michael Jones, Washington Athletic Club Pastry Chef.

Metropolitan Grill

820 2nd Avenue
Seattle, Washington 98104
(206) 624-3287

Located in the heart of Seattle's downtown financial and business center, "The Met" is very simply the best steak house in town.

Nobody could describe the experience better than *Seattle Times* restaurant critic John Hinterberger. "A downtown business person's restaurant for lunch which becomes a steak house for dinner – arguably the best in town."

The Metropolitan Grill features dry-cured and 28-day aging of its meat. The beef is carefully broiled over the "iron wood of the world," imported mesquite charcoal, to further enhance its flavor. The sight of a fabulous Porterhouse, Delmonico or Chateaubriand for two, never was more appealing or flavorful. And there's always fresh King Salmon, Veal Parmigiana, or extra thick Veal Chops to tempt your taste buds.

While beef is the mainstay of the Met, the lunch menu features the freshest pastas, salads, fish and homemade soups. The dinner menu is enhanced by the latest catch of Northwest Seafood.

Rated one of the Top Ten Steak Houses in the country, the Metropolitan Grill continues to be Seattle's favorite Steak House.

New York Peppercorn Steak

Serves 2

2 16-oz New York steaks	⅓ lb celery
1 cup cracked black pepper	⅓ lb tomatoes
2 lbs veal bones	½ sm can green peppercorns
¼ cup burgundy	¼ cup brandy
⅓ lb mushrooms	pinch cayenne pepper
⅓ lb onion	2 cups brown roux*

Place bones, ¼ cup cracked pepper, burgundy, mushrooms, onion, celery, and tomatoes in roasting pan and roast at 350° for 3 hours. Add 1 gallon water and cook over low heat for eight hours. Strain. Reduce stock ⅔ and thicken with brown roux. Finish with brandy and green peppercorns. Add cayenne to taste.

Press cracked black pepper into New York steak. Broil to desired doneness and top with a generous amount of sauce.

* Brown roux: browned mixture of equal parts butter and flour. Used as thickening.

Cheddar Cheese and Beer Sauce

Makes 2 quarts

2 Tbsp chopped parsley	12 oz Henry's beer
1 Tbsp chopped green onion	1 Tbsp granulated garlic
1 cup butter, melted	1 Tbsp white pepper
1 cup flour	1 Tbsp Worcestershire sauce
1 qt cream	1 lb grated cheddar cheese

Combine parsley, green onion and butter in 4 quart sauce pot and cook over medium heat for 5 minutes. Add flour and cook for 10 minutes. Add cream, beer, garlic, pepper and Worcestershire sauce. Bring to a boil and simmer for 15 minutes.

Add cheese and whisk until melted. Serve over baked potato.

Tenderloin Steak Sandwich

Serves 5

1 lb beef tenderloin medallions
5 kaiser dollar-sized buns
1 oz steak seasoning
5 Tbsp grade AA butter

1 tsp fresh minced garlic
½ tsp chopped parsley
½ minced green onion
½ tsp granulated onion

Soften butter. Add minced garlic, parsley, green onion and granulated onion to butter and blend thoroughly. Butter kaiser dollar buns. Season tenderloin medallions, to taste. Mesquite broil 1 to 2 minutes per side (preferred rare to medium rare).

Serve hot on Kaiser buns.

MILLSTONE®
WHOLE BEAN COFFEES

729 100th St SE
Everett, Washingon 98208
(206) 347-3995
1-800-SAY-JAVA

Millstone – roasted fresh in the Pacific Northwest. For some added summertime fun, try out these favorite Millstone recipes.

Millstone Java Shake*

Makes 2 tall or 4 short servings

1 c extra strength chilled
  Millstone Bed & Breakfast
  Blend coffee®

3 Tbsp chocolate syrup (or add
  to taste)

5 c vanilla ice cream

Blend coffee, syrup, and ice cream in blender until smooth. For best results, pour into chilled glasses, let stand a minute. Top with whipped cream and serve.

*Millstone® Java Shake®

Millstone Mocha Punch

Serves 35

1 qt of your favorite dark-roasted
  Millstone® coffee (chilled &
  double strength)
1 qt chocolate ice cream
1 qt vanilla ice cream
1 c whipping cream

¼ tsp salt
½ c sugar
¼ tsp almond extract
½ tsp vanilla
½ tsp nutmeg
¼ tsp cinnamon, optional

Pour chilled coffee into a punch bowl. Add walnut-sized
chunks of ice cream. Whip cream, adding salt, almond extract
and vanilla; fold into punch. Sprinkle with nutmeg and
cinnamon.

Millstone Vanilla 'Cappuccino'

Serves 2

Here's a way to make delicious cappuccino without a home espresso maker.

1 c milk

2 tsp packed light brown sugar

1½ c (12 oz) strong, brewed
  Millstone Bed & Breakfast
  Blend® coffee

½ tsp pure vanilla extract

ground cinnamon or cocoa

In a small saucepan, combine the milk and vanilla. Scald the milk. Remove from the heat. Cover and let the milk steep for 5 minutes.

If you like your coffee sweetened, stir sugar into the milk. Reheat the milk briefly over high heat until steaming. Transfer the milk to a blender. Whirl milk until frothy, at least 45 seconds. Half-fill 2 warmed coffee mugs or cups with hot coffee. Add the hot milk, dividing it evenly, and spoon a little bit of the froth into the cups. Sprinkle the cinnamon or cocoa lightly on top.

Raspberry Java Jumble Bars*

Make 24 squares

2 c all-purpose flour
1 tsp baking powder
¼ tsp baking soda
1¾ c quick-cooking oatmeal
1 c brown sugar, firmly packed

¼ c Northwest Select™ coffee, brewed and double-strength
¾ c butter or margarine (1½ sticks), cut into small cubes
1½ c raspberry jam

Preheat oven to 350 degrees. Sift together flour, baking powder and baking soda into a medium bowl. Stir in oatmeal, brown sugar and coffee. With a pastry blender or 2 knives, cut in the butter or margarine until mixture resembles coarse crumbs. Place about ⅔ of mixture in an ungreased 11" x 7" baking dish. With fingers, press out evenly. Spread with raspberry jam. Cover evenly with remaining mixture. Press down lightly. Bake in preheated oven 30 to 35 minutes or until just lightly browned. Cool in pan. Cut into 1¾ inch squares.

*Raspberry Java Jumble Bars™

Blazing Barbeque Sauce

Makes 1½ cups sauce

1 c tomato ketchup

5 Tbsp butter

⅓ c Millstone Northwest Select™ coffee, brewed and double-strength

3 Tbsp Worcestershire sauce

1 to 2 Tbsp pure ground hot chile or crushed red chile

1 Tbsp dark brown sugar, packed

In a 2-quart saucepan, combine ingredients and allow to simmer, uncovered, over medium heat for 10 to 15 minutes. Set aside or refrigerate, covered, until ready to barbecue. Great on chicken, pork, or beef ribs.

Hint: adjust the "temperature" of this sauce to your taste by using more or less chile spice. Try a tray of "Blazing" chicken wings for your next get-together.

MISTY'S

Red Lion Hotel, Bellevue
300 112th Ave. S.E.
Bellevue, Washington 98004
(206) 450-4154

In the past ten years, Misty's has become "the place for special occasion dining" in Bellevue, featuring artful tableside flambee cooking prepared by our expert staff. Although Misty's specializes in tableside preparations, we also offer a complete lunch and dinner menu highlighting Northwest regional favorites.

A spectacular Sunday brunch buffet is served every Sunday.

Steak Diane

Serves 2

2 8-oz beef tenderloins
½ oz olive oil
1 clove garlic, minced
1 bulb shallots, minced
3 lg mushrooms, sliced
1 tsp Dijon mustard
1 Tbsp Worcestershire sauce

6 oz Bordelaise sauce*
1½ oz sour cream
1 oz red wine
1½ oz brandy
salt to taste
black pepper to taste

Add olive oil to a large saute pan on medium-high heat. Add garlic and shallots to pan and saute lightly. Add steaks and sear until brown on both sides, adding 2 drops of Worcestershire sauce to each. Add mushrooms to pan, and saute them with red wine and the remainder of the Worcestershire sauce.

Remove pan from heat and push ingredients to one side. Add brandy to exposed spot in pan and ignite with a match.

Add Bordelaise sauce and bring to a boil. Lower the temperature and stir in sour cream to the sauce. Place steaks on plates and top with mushroom/sauce mixture.

Note: Bordelaise sauce is a reduction of red wine, shallots, thyme, bay leaf and black pepper. Add beef stock and reduce further. Finish with a roux (reduced 1 part flour and 1 part butter) to give a velvety texture.

10800 NE 8th Street, Suite 105
Bellevue, Washington 98004
(206) 454-6024

Pagliacci (pronounced pah-lee-yacht-chee) means clowns in Italian. Pizzeria Paglicci is an East Coast or Neapolitan style pizzeria which first appeared in the U-District in 1979 and featured "pizza-by-the-slice." The pizzeria was quite popular and led to the opening of additional pizzerias in the greater Seattle area. Pagliacci is not a chain or a franchise.

Our goal isn't to be the biggest, but it is to be the best. Pagliacci has been rated "the Best Pizza" by Seattle Weekly readers since 1986. Aside from featuring fast, fresh pizza-by-the-slice, what makes our pizza special? We hand-spin every pizza dough, use 100% whole milk mozzarella cheese and cook the pizza on hot bricks like it's done it Italy.

Pizza Dough Centioli

Makes 3 thin or 2 thick crusts

2 c warm water (105-115 degrees)

1 env dry yeast

1 Tbsp salt

2 Tbsp olive oil

5½ c flour (preferably unbleached
  bread or high-protein)

Pour ¼ c of the warm water into a measuring cup, sprinkle in yeast and stir to dissolve.

In a large bowl combine the remaining 1¾ cups of warm water, salt, olive oil and 3 cups of the flour and mix well by hand. Add the yeast mixture and gradually work in the remaining 2½ cups of flour.

Knead the dough for about 10 minutes. It should be firm, but elastic. Shape into a ball and turn into a greased bowl to coat surface of dough. Cover bowl and put in a warm place, such as an electric oven with the light turned on, until doubled in size, about 1 hour.

Knead dough again and then let it rest for about 10 minutes. To form crusts divide the dough into three pieces if you want three 15-inch thin crusts or into two pieces if you want two 15-inch thick crusts.

For a lighter crust, toss the dough in the air a few times, then finish spreading it out with your fingers on greased pans.

Lightly brush dough with olive oil and tomato sauce. If making a thick crust, let it rise about another 30 minutes before topping with your favorite ingredients and cheeses.

Bake pizzas in a preheated 450 degree oven until edges are well-browned and the cheese is bubbly. Watch closely to make sure they do not burn.

Pollo Pizza

Makes 1 small pizza

3 oz chunk chicken breast   1 tsp garlic
1 oz sun-dried tomatoes   1 pizza dough
2 oz crumbled goat cheese   1 oz olive oil

Saute chicken breast with salt and pepper in oil until almost done and deglaze with white wine. Chop tomatoes with chicken until about the size of peas. Moisten all with oil from sun-dried tomatoes.

Pull out dough and moisten with oil. Spread garlic over oil. Take tomato/chicken mixture and spread on dough. Crumble goat cheese over all. Bake.

Calzone

4 oz prosciutto ham, thinly sliced

½ c ricotta cheese

1 c mozzarella cheese, shredded

¼ c black olives, sliced

1 egg, boiled and coarsely chopped

6 artichoke hearts, crumbled

1 pizza dough

Stretch out dough. Spread ricotta, mozzarella, black olives, artichoke hearts and egg on half of dough. Lay prosciutto over all. Fold, seal with a fork. Bake in 450 degree oven or until golden brown. Brush with olive oil and cut into serving pieces.

SEAFOOD GRILL

3014 3rd Ave N.
Seattle, Washington 98109
(206) 284-3000

Ponti Seafood Grill is located on the ship canal just west of the Fremont Bridge in a European-like setting, with views of the Fremont, Aurora, and ship canal bridges. Hence the name ("ponti" means "bridges" in Italian).

Owners Jim Malevitsis and Richard Malia, along with chef Alvin Binuya, created a menu with broad appeal and a wide variety of preparations, taking the best of many different ethnic cuisines.

Sashimi Salad

Makes 1 entree or 4 starter salads

4 oz sahimi grade tuna,
  thinly sliced

⅓ c seeded & sliced cucumber

¼ c Roma tomatoes, sliced in
  strips

2 Tbsp finely chopped green onion

⅓ c ginger-orange dressing
  (recipe follows)

2 c loosely packed mixed wild
  greens

1 c fried won ton wrapper, cut
  into strips prior to deep frying

In a large bowl, mix tuna, cucumber, tomato, green onion and dressing. Allow to marinate 2-3 minutes. (If you wish to prepare ahead, this mixture can sit up to 30 minutes.)

Just prior to serving, add the wild greens and fried won ton skins, and toss well. Arrange in a tall mound on a plate garnished with lettuce leaves and radish sprouts.

Garlic-Parmesan Mashed Potatoes

Serves 4-6

3 lbs peeled yellow fin or
   Yukon Gold potatoes
1½ c whipping cream

¼ c butter
2 Tbsp chopped garlic
1 c grated parmesan

Simmer potatoes in water until easily pierced with a knife (about 40-50 minutes). Meanwhile, heat cream, butter, and garlic to a simmer. Strain potatoes and place in a large bowl. Mash with a stiff whisk until just mashed. Add parmesan cheese and cream mixture to potatoes and mix until blended.

Do not overmix as this will create gluey spuds. Season to taste with salt and pepper.

Ginger-Orange Soy Dressing
for Sashimi Salad

¼ c orange juice

1 tsp grated ginger

½ tsp orange zest

⅓ c soy sauce

¼ c rice wine vinegar

½ tsp black pepper

2 Tbsp sesame oil

½ c peanut oil

In food processor combine all ingredients, except oils, and blend well.

With machine running, slowly drizzle both oils into mixture. Refrigerate.

You'll Feel Rich With The Taste of Italy.

Virginia at 2nd Avenue
2000 2nd Avenue
Seattle, Washington 98121
(206) 441-4313

The Poor Italian Cafe is a well-lit and lively Italian-American restaurant located on the border between downtown Seattle and the Denny regrade. This site makes the Poor Italian within easy walking distance of most downtown offices, hotels, theatres and the Pike Place Market.

The Cafe's food is quality authentic Italian fare with American portions and tastes constantly kept in mind. It is prepared by Italians who insist on maintaining the integrity of the old Italian ways of cooking.

Service is friendly, courteous, and efficient. Everyone working at the Poor Italian Cafe looks forward to welcoming you soon.

Chicken Marsala

Serves 2

2 6-oz boneless chicken breasts
1 oz olive oil
2 oz sliced mushrooms
½ oz copaccola ham (spicy)
1 oz sliced roasted red peppers
3 oz marsala

3 oz chicken stock
2 oz butter
chopped parsley
flour for dredging
seasoning salt

Dredge chicken breasts in flour. Shake off excess, then season.

Heat oil in saute pan and brown both sides of chicken evenly. Drain off oil and add mushrooms, roasted red peppers and copaccola. Deglaze pan with marsala; reduce sauce a little and add chicken stock. Continue to reduce sauce until chicken is cooked. Check for seasoning and finish sauce with butter.

Transfer chicken breast to plate. Top with sauce and sprinkle freshly chopped parsley to garnish. Serve with pasta, potato or rice and steamed vegetables.

Calamari Livornese

Serves 2

6 oz squid, cleaned, cut into rings
   (tentacles included)
2 oz mushrooms, sliced
2 oz onions, diced
2 oz olive oil
1 tsp garlic

pinch of red pepper flakes
pinch of oregano
¼ lemon
12 oz marinara sauce
buttered fettucine

Heat saute pan. Add oil, heat and add mushrooms and onions. Cook until slightly colored.

Add calamari, garlic and oregano and saute until squid is cooked (the opaque appearance of the squid disappears when it's cooked). Season and drain liquids. Squeeze the juice of ¼ lemon over the top and add marinara sauce.

Heat through and serve on a bed of buttered fettuccine and steamed vegetables on the side.

PRESTON
WINE CELLARS

502 E Vineyard Drive
Pasco, Washington 99301
(509) 545-1990

Preston Wine Cellars, located in the fertile irrigated farmlands of Washington State's Columbia Basin, is one of the Pacific Northwest's most promising wine growing endeavors. Eastern Washington, climatically similar to Northern Europe, is fast gaining recognition as a major production area for wine grapes of exceptional varietal character and balance. Bill and Joann Preston were among the pioneer families who early on recognized the potential of this unexploited area. In 1972 the first vineyard of 50 acres was planted and was increased by 131 acres in 1979.

In the spring of 1976 ground was broken for the winery building and the first crush got underway in late September of that same year. By the fall of 1977 Preston's dream was completed by adding a tasting bar, retail sales room and gift shop. The elevated tasting-room, nestled in the estate vineyards, is uniquely decorated in cedar with a handcrafted bar and personalized furniture created by Brent Preston. Visitors may sip four wines of the 14 award-winning wines on the tasting bar daily, either inside or outside on the over-hanging deck, while enjoying a panoramic view of the vineyards and surrounding countryside.

You may wish to go on a self-guided tour by meandering through hallways containing awards from present and past years and viewing rooms which overlook rows of stainless steel tanks, French oak cooperage, and the mechanized bottling line.

The Prestons and staff cordially invite you to visit the winery year around. We are open daily from 10:00 am, to 5:30 pm, except major holidays. We are located 5 miles north of Pasco on Highway 395. Watch for our sign on the east side of the highway.

Beef Salami

Makes 4 logs

4 lbs ground beef
1 tsp onion powder
1½ tsp garlic powder
2 tsp peppercorns
2 Tbsp liquid smoke

¼ c "Morton Tender Quick" (curing salt)
2 tsp "Mrs. Dash" salt-free seasoning
2 tsp whole mustard seeds
¼ c Preston Cabernet Sauvignon

Mix well in large bowl and leave in refrigerator for 24 hours. Then shape into 4 logs and bake for 4 hours at 225 degrees, turning logs ¼ turn every hour. Freezes well.

Bill's Pork Roast & Wine

Serves 4

4-5 lbs boneless pork roast
  butterfly (flat)
1 or 2 sliced red apples
3 Tbsp brown sugar, sprinkled

4 Tbsp honey, drizzled all over
4 Tbsp butter
1 c Preston Desert Blossom

Re-roll roast and marinate in Preston Desert Blossom for 2 hours. Cook on rotisserie (in basket) for 1 hour or until done. (Baste with wine every 15 minutes).

OR

Bake at 325 degrees on an open rack in oven until done. Turn and brown in last minutes.

Chocolate Cabernet Cake

Makes 1 cake

1 pkg chocolate fudge cake mix
1½ c sour cream
¾ c vegetable oil
1 c Preston Cabernet Sauvignon

2 eggs, beaten
1 4-oz pkg instant chocolate
pudding

Preheat oven to 350 degrees. Grease and flour bundt pan. Combine all ingredients and bake for about 45 minutes. Dust with powdered sugar or serve with raspberries.

RAINIER
The Only Beer.

3100 Airport Way South
Seattle, Washington 98134
(206) 622-2600

Free Public Tours are available, Monday-Friday, 1:00-6:00PM.

Beer, for all its other attributes, is an excellent seasoning agent. It imparts a subtlety all its own to a variety of dishes, blending harmoniously with other flavors. Beer enhances the natural richness of meats and vegetables when used in place of water as a simmering or braising agent. It tenderizes meats, fish and shellfish, and adds richness to sauces and gravies.

Cheese and beer are particularly well suited to each other, in the kitchen as well as on the party table.

Perhaps the most surprising attribute of beer in cooking is the lightness and delicate richness it imparts in baking. Biscuits, pancakes, and bread all benefit from the substitution of beer for other liquids in many recipes.

Beer Cheese

Makes 1 quart

1 lb med sharp cheese (approx 4
  c ground)
1 tsp garlic salt
2 tsp minced onion
1 tsp dry mustard

dash tabasco
1 tsp Worcestershire
1 Tbsp butter
8 oz Rainier beer

Grind or grate cheese. Place all ingredients except beer in mixer bowl. Gradually add beer and beat until smooth and fluffy. Store in covered container in refrigerator. Serve at room temperature with crackers or dark bread.

Hot German Potato Salad

Serves 8

6 med potatoes

6 slices bacon, cooked &
  crumbled

1½ tsp minced onion

½ c chopped celery

Dressing:

¼ c melted butter

¼ c flour

1 tsp salt

⅛ tsp dry mustard

1½ Tbsp sugar

¼ c Rainier Beer

3 Tbsp vinegar

¼ tsp tabasco

1 Tbsp chopped parsley

Cook potatoes until tender but firm. Peel and dice while still warm. Add bacon, celery and onion. Mix butter and dry ingredients into a smooth paste. Gradually add liquids and cook, stirring constantly, until mixture thickens and comes to a boil.

Pour mixture over potatoes, sprinkle with parsley and mix lightly. Heat in 350 degree oven for 20 minutes.

Rainier Barbeque Sauce

2 Tbsp cooking oil
1 onion, chopped fine
1 6-oz can tomato paste
1 12-oz can Rainier beer
1 Tbsp vinegar
1 Tbsp Worcestershire
dash tabasco

1 Tbsp sugar
1 Tbsp chili powder
1 tsp salt
1 tsp garlic salt
1 tsp dry mustard
1 tsp paprika
1 tsp Accent

Brown onions in oil. Mix and add remaining ingredients. Simmer ½ hour. Pour over 2 pounds weiners. Heat in 350 degree oven for 20 minutes.

GOOD FOOD • GOOD DRINKS • GOOD FRIENDS

9635 Des Moines Memorial Drive
Seattle, Washington 98108
(206) 763-7428

Rascal's is owned and operated by two restauranteurs, B.J. Wakkuri and Rick Colgan. Both were trained at WSU in the hotel and restaurant program and have survived the local restaurant scene. Under their direction, Rascal's boasts "only the best in casual dining and hospitality." The menu features honest local and American cuisine and is always guaranteed to be "pretty darn good." Here are three of our most sought-after recipes. Happy cooking.

Rascal's Whiskey BBQ Sauce

Makes 1 gallon

½ lb butter

½ lb brown sugar

1 c molasses

1 c honey

1 c red wine vinegar

1 c Worcestershire

1½ oz Tabasco

2½ oz A-1 sauce

6 oz Kentucky whiskey

1 tsp black pepper

¼ c lemon juice

1 Tbsp minced garlic

⅛ c sugar

¼ c salt

1 qt beef stock

⅛ c liquid smoke

¼ oz cayenne pepper

33 oz tomato sauce

9 oz tomato paste

Spice bag ingredients:

2 bay leaves

½ tsp marjoram

½ tsp rosemary

½ tsp basil

½ tsp cloves

Combine butter and brown sugar. Carmelize over low heat for 15 minutes. Add the rest of the ingredients except tomato paste. Simmer covered for two hours, stirring regularly. Add tomato paste and simmer half an hour longer. Remove spice bag and let sauce cool.

The sauce has a 6 week shelf life.

Rascal's Whiskey BBQ Tartar Sauce

Makes 8 2-oz servings

2 c Rascal's Whiskey BBQ Sauce
4 Tbsp prepared horseradish

2 Tbsp lemon juice
3 Tbsp dill relish

Blend together well and serve with any smoked fish or your favorite BBQ fish items. This recipe uses the first Whiskey BBQ Sauce as a master sauce and works especially well with BBQ fish of all kinds. The sauce was developed for Rascal's Northwest-style smoked salmon fish and chips.

Smoked Salmon Fish & Chips

Serves 8

1½ to 2 lb cod filet

½ lb flour

8 oz Red Hook ESB or any favorite beer

4 oz half and half

2 c Panko breading mix

2 c sour dough bread crumbs

8 oz sliced Nova smoked salmon

Cut cod on bias into 2 oz filets about palm size. Slice a pocket into the filet and lay in ½ oz smoked salmon and close up. Dip in flour both sides.

Combine eggs, beer and half and half in a large bowl. Blend well. Dip floured filet into egg wash. Dip egg-washed filet into a blending of the two bread crumbs.

Dust off and deep fry in lite canola oil at 350 degrees for 4 to 6 minutes.

Serve with the whiskey BBQ Tartar Sauce.

Mamma Melina

RISTORANTE ITALIANO

4759 Roosevelt Way NE
Seattle, Washington 98105
(206) 632-2271

Two years ago the Varchetta family moved from Naples to Seattle.

Salvio and Roberto opened "Buongusto" on Queen Anne. Soon afterwards, Leo opened "Mamma Melina" in the University District.

Teamed with his mother and father, they provide a cultural experience unique to Seattle. Pasquale with his beautiful paintings and singing, Melina's fifty years cooking experience and Leo's extensive knowledge of Italian wines bring you the sounds, aromas and flavors of Southern Italy.

With Melina in the kitchen is Chef James Best. Together they prepare the freshest local and finest Italian ingredients in traditional Neapolitan style.

Calamari Affogati

Serves 4

⅓ c olive oil
2 cloves garlic, coarsely chopped
4 sprigs Italian parsley
3 sm Roma tomatoes

1 lb calamari, cleaned and cut into rings
salt to taste
crushed red pepper flakes to taste

Saute garlic in olive oil until toasty brown, taking care that it doesn't burn.

Add chopped Roma tomatoes, cover and simmer 3 minutes. Add calamari, salt, red pepper and parsley. Toss, then cover and simmer 3 minutes.

Serve as antipasti or with spaghetti. This dish represents the best of Capri, Naples and Ischia.

Paglia e Fieno

Serves 4

1 lb fresh spaghetti, green
  and yellow
¼ lb shitake mushrooms
1 c baby peas
4 baby Cipellini onions

¼ lb ham, diced ⅜" squares
1½ c heavy cream
1 c parmesano reggiano, shredded
salt and pepper to taste

Heat olive oil in heavy gauge pan, saute onion, then add ham, peas and mushrooms. Season with salt and pepper. Add cream and reduce 3 minutes on low heat.

Cook fresh spaghetti al dente in salted water. Drain pasta. Add pasta to sauce and toss with parmesan. Serve immediately.

Fresh Prawn Antipasti

with Lemon Aoli

Serves 8

about 40 fresh spot prawns
celery stalk
¼ c salt
2 Tbsp peppercorns
1 whole egg
2 egg yolks

2 tsp sugar
1 tsp salt
1 c light olive oil
1 oz white wine vinegar
4 oz fresh lemon juice
3 Tbsp fresh chopped garlic

Simmer celery and peppercorns and ¼ cup salt in 6 cups water for 10 minutes in a broad, shallow pan. Add prawns and cook lightly for only 1 to 2 minutes. Strain and cool.

For aoli: in pan, saute garlic in olive oil until toasty brown. Set aside. In blender, whip eggs and yolks. Add sugar and salt. Add vinegar and lemon juice. Very slowly, drip in oil. Continue blending at high speed until consistency of mayonnaise. If it separates, remove and start again with 1 egg. Add garlic to aoli.

Peel prawns and serve cold with aoli.

ristorante **Stresa**

2220 Carillon Point
Kirkland, Washington 98033
(206) 889-9006

Stresa is a beautiful little city on the Lake Maggiore, for years the favorite place for European tourists. Stresa Restaurant opened at Carillon Point on Lake Washington in 1989 and is already one of the best places on the Eastside. The restaurant is located on the south side of the plaza and overlooks the marina.

Its menu, the staff, and the outside patios make Stresa a sure bet, especially in sunny weather. Benvenuti.

Tonno Agrodolce
Tuna in a Sweet & Sour Sauce

Serves 6

2½ lbs fresh tuna, cut into small
  rectangular pieces

olive oil

flour

red onion, cut in sm slices

vinegar

sugar

salt

Toss tuna pieces in flour and add salt. Then fry in hot oil for a few minutes (don't let the tuna color too much). Take pieces out and put them aside. Fry the onion in leftover oil until it becomes a golden color and add salt. Sprinkle with a good vinegar and a little sugar and add the tuna again. Let the tuna sit in the sauce for a couple of mintues more and serve.

Risotto con Frutti di Mare
Seafood Risotto

Serves 6

1 lb Arborio rice

2 lbs clams

1 lb mussels

4 oz shrimp (shelled, parboiled, and diced)

4 oz mushrooms (cooked and sliced)

1 onion (finely chopped)

1 Tbsp chopped parsley

3 Tbsp white wine

2 oz olive oil

2 oz butter

salt and pepper

Wash shellfish, place in a large pot with wine and over high heat, steam until they open (discard any that don't open). Remove shellfish. Strain and reserve cooking liquid. Place oil in a smaller pot and over medium heat, saute onion until blond.

Add the juice obtained from cooking shellfish, previously strained, and reduce to half the volume. Add the rice, mix well, add a quart of boiling water. After ten mintues add the clams, mussels, shrimp and mushrooms. Season with salt and pepper.

Stir in additional water a few tablespoons at a time as the rice gets thicker and dryer. When cooked al dente add the butter and chopped parsley. Serve right away.

San Carlos Restaurant

FINE FOOD AND DRINK OF THE SOUTHWEST

279 Madison Avenue
Bainbridge Island, Washington 98110
(206) 842-1999

San Carlos Restaurant opened in May 1984, and was voted Best Restaurant in Kitsap County in 1987 by a county-wide readership poll of the Tideland's publishing company. San Carlos serves the finest Southwestern foods in the Northwest, and is a great little excursion from greater Seattle on a Washington State ferry, when you have guests visiting or you just want to get out of the city. It is an easy 35-minute boat ride from downtown Seattle to the Winslow terminal, and the restaurant is a pleasant hike through the local village. Please call 842-7499 for directions and reservations.

We feature mesquite smoked specialties, Sonoran style seafood and Mexican food, daily special entrees from the Southwestern states and fresh and tropical margaritas, San Carlos Restaurant's staff and management are very excited to host your visit this summer.

Scallops San Carlos

Serves 6

2 to 3 lbs fresh Mexican Bay
  scallops
1 lb bay shrimp
1 lb unsalted butter or high
  quality soy margarine
  (Willow Run brand)
½ Tbsp garlic, minced or pureed
1 tomato, diced

green chilis, diced
⅓ - ½ c white cooking wine
salsa fresca
2 oz herbed cheese
1 fresh lemon
salt
cilantro

Place the butter or margarine in a large saucepan and melt. Add diced tomato, green chilies, and garlic. Saute over medium heat until tomatoes are soft. Add two 3-oz ladles of salsa fresca to butter sauce, and whip until combined
Add bay scallops and bay shrimps to butter sauce, and saute until scallops are tender and cooked through (don't overcook).

Just as scallops finish cooking, add the herbed goat cheese and melt into the butter sauce. If sauce needs to be thickened just a bit, add a pinch of flour or spoonful of roux, and stir.

Garnish with fresh cilantro, guacamole, queso blanco, or freshly grated Parmesan cheese and a lemon wedge.

Excellent served with Spanish rice, black beans and flour tortillas.

148

Stuffed Avocado Salad San Carlos

Serves 1

bed of salad greens
your favorite salad garnishes
½ ripe avocado, peeled & pitted
stuffings: bay shrimp, Dungeness
 .crab, cold poached scallops,
 smoked chicken, etc.

Sauce: ½ c mayonnaise
½ c sour cream
⅔ c San Carlos salsa fresca
pinch salt
squeeze lemon juice
½ tsp pureed garlic

Place sauce ingredients in mixing bowl and whisk together. Thin with water if necessary.

Center ½ avocado with your choice of stuffing on salad greens. Garnish to taste and spoon salsa/mayonnaise sauce over stuffed avocado. Top with queso blanco or grated Parmesan cheese.

Seattle Salsa is a locally made sauce designed to be enjoyed with a variety of foods. Combining traditional ingredients with a touch of honey, this salsa adds new dimension to an honored Mexican tradition. Whether enjoyed as a dip with nachos, a topping on your favorite hamburger, or as a dressing to spice up a salad, we hope you will try this unique salsa.

Mexican Manicotti

½ lb lean ground beef

1 c refried beans

½ tsp crushed oregano

½ tsp ground cumin

8 uncooked manicotti shells

8 oz Seattle Salsa

1 c grated cheese

1½ c water

Brown meat. Mix beef, beans and spices and stuff mixture into manicotti shells. Arrange in a 10x6x2" baking dish. Combine salsa with water. Pour over shells, cover and bake at 325 degrees for about 1½ hours.

Remove and top with 1 cup grated cheese. Return to oven just until cheese melts. Remove and serve. Top with sour cream, chopped green onions, chopped ripe olives and Seattle Salsa.

Halibut Salsa Style

2 lbs halibut steaks

1 c coarsely chopped onion

3 sm zucchini, sliced

3 cloves garlic, minced

6 Tbsp olive oil, divided

2 Tbsp chopped parsley or cilantro

2 Tbsp lemon juice

8 oz Seattle Salsa

Salt and pepper the halibut steaks. Saute zucchini, onion and garlic in 2 Tbsp oil. Remove from pan. Add remaining oil and saute halibut until brown on both sides.

Return vegetables to pan and add lemon juice, salsa and parsley or cilantro. Heat briefly.

Seattle Salsa Lasagne

Serves 4-6

1 bunch fresh spinach	10 oz mozzarella cheese
1 red bell pepper	1 15 oz carton ricotta
1 onion	2 sheets fresh pasta
2-3 cloves garlic	
10 oz Jack cheese	1 16 oz jar Seattle Salsa

Wash spinach and spin dry. Saute pepper and onion, sliced julienne, with minced garlic in olive oil. Set aside. Grate and mix cheeses. Thin ricotta with 2 Tbsp cream or milk. Preheat oven to 350 degrees.

In 9x13 pan begin layering, in this order: ½ cup salsa, sheet of pasta, half the spinach, half the onion mixture, half the ricotta, half the grated cheese, ¾ cup salsa. Then repeat the pasta, spinach, onion mixture and ricotta. Finish with half the remaining cheese, ¾ cup salsa, and finally, the remaining cheese.

Bake for thirty minutes. Let set five minutes. Cut to serving portions. Serve with a sprig of cilantro and cherry tomatoes for a festive and delicious entree.

Rustic Euro-Italian Restaurant & Bar
2043 Eastlake Avenue East
Seattle, Washington
(206) 323-0807

Involtini di Melanzane
Rolled & Stuffed Eggplant

Serves 6

2 lg eggplant

3 c ricotta cheese

1 bunch fresh spinach

vegetable oil for frying

1 tsp red chile pepper flakes

dash nutmeg and cinnamon

4 eggs

1 c flour seasoned with salt
  & pepper

3 c traditional marinara sauce

Cut the eggplant lengthwise in ¼" slices. Flour and dip sliced eggplant in a eggwash. Saute immediately in hot oil and drain. While eggplant is cooling, begin to mix stuffing. Julienne spinach leaves, and blend with ricotta and 1 egg. Add chile peppers, nutmeg, cinnamon and salt and pepper.

Divide ricotta filling into six parts. Fill each slice of eggplant with 1 part of ricotta stuffing and roll into a tube.

Grease an 8" square pan and cover the bottom with half of the marinara sauce. Lay eggplant tubes in pan and cover with the remaining sauce. Cover with foil and bake at 325 degrees for 20 minutes.

Penne Rossa

Serves 2-3

12 Roma tomatoes
4 oz heavy cream
3 oz smoked mozzarella cheese, at room temperature
7 basil leaves
12 oz fresh penne pasta

Saute tomatoes dry in a braising pan until they are soft, then put them through a food mill and let cool. Return tomatoes to braising pan and add cream and salt and pepper to taste and reduce.

Boil pasta and add to reduced tomatoes and cream sauce. Tear basil leaves in thirds and add to sauce. Finish by tossing with smoked mozzarella. Garnish with basil leaves and serve immediately.

Spuma Cioccolata

Serves 10-12

24 oz semi-sweet guittard
 chocolate
15 eggs, separated
3 c heavy cream

¼ c sugar
1 shot of espresso
2 tsp dark rum

Melt chocolate in a double boiler. Separate eggs, whip whites and refrigerate. Whip yolks until they are light in color, adding sugar, espresso and rum. Add melted chocolate to egg mixture.

Whip heavy cream and add to yolks and chocolate. Finish by adding chilled egg whites. Refrigerate for several hours before serving.

Setaté

Setate Foods
P.O. Box 22396
Seattle, Washington 98122-0396
(206) 720-6220

To most Ethiopians, the word setate conjures up culinary anticipation and images that delight the appetite (a setate is a large clay pot used for cooking).

On the other hand, the word kulet represents hours of undivided attention to what is cooking in the setate. Kulet is a base red pepper sauce. It contains all the main ingredients and spices to make any type of wot (red pepper sauce) and can be used in various recipes.

The additional spices in the following recipes are optional and are only meant to enhance the particular dish that is being cooked. The secret to Ethiopian cooking lies in the spices, which have been sun-dried, finely ground in wooden mortars and cleverly combined.

Timing of the addition of these spices when cooking is of the utmost importance since different spices retain their optimum flavor at different stages of cooking. Although cooking is individual and requires unbridled imagination, it also requires the knowledge of certain basics in the various cuisines.

The Ethiopian foods that most Americans have come to know and love, has just been made easier to cook right at home.

In making kulet, Setate Foods has taken away the time-consuming portion of cooking wot, so you are free to use your imagination in creating dish after dish.

What makes kulet truly special is its versatility.

Bederjan (Baked Eggplant)

Serves 8

1 c kulet	1 tsp ginger
½ c tomato paste	½ tsp black pepper
¼ c vegetable oil	1 tsp cinnamon
2 stalks green onions, chopped	1 lg eggplant, sliced
2 c water	1 med green pepper
1 tsp garlic	parmesan cheese

In a medium saucepan heat kulet, tomato paste, oil and green onions. Simmer for about 15 to 20 minutes, adding water as needed.

Add remaining spices (items six through nine) and simmer for an additional 5 minutes.

In a baking dish, layer ingredients in the following order: sauce (spoon just enough to cover bottom of baking dish); eggplant slices; sauce; sprinkle of parmesan; sliced green pepper; more slices eggplant; sauce; remaining parmesan on top. Bake at 375 degrees for about 25 minutes or until eggplant is cooked.

Kek Wot
Yellow Split Peas in Red Pepper Sauce

Serves 8

1½ c yellow split peas
½ c vegetable oil
4½ c water for boiling peas
6 c water

½ tsp cardamom
salt & pepper to taste
kulet, 16 oz jar

Boil yellow split peas in 4½ c of water for 15 minutes. Strain.

Pour kulet and oil in medium saucepan and heat to boil. Reduce heat and simmer for 15 minutes. Add strained split peas. Simmer together for 40 to 45 minutes, adding water as needed.

Add cardamom, salt and pepper, and let simmer for about 5 minutes longer.

This dish should have the consistency of sloppy Joe's. It can be eaten with bread, rice, or injera (Ethiopian flat spongy bread).

Doro Wot

Chicken in Red Pepper Sauce

Serves 5

16 oz jar kulet

¼ c butter

1 chicken, cut up

2 med limes

½ c water

¼ c dry red wine, optional

½ tsp black pepper

½ tsp cardamom

salt to taste

4-6 hard boiled eggs

Thoroughly wash chicken and remove visible fat from skin. Soak chicken in a large bowl of clean water and the juice of the lime, leaving the lime rind in the boil.

Pour kulet in a large saucepan and heat. Add butter and cook for 15 minutes. Rinse chicken and pat dry. Add chicken in sauce and cook until chicken is done (about 30-40 minutes), adding water and/or red wine as needed.

Add cardamom, pepper and salt to taste. Add hard boiled eggs to sauce. Serve hot on injera or rice.

Kulet can be purchased from Setate Foods or from specialty food stores. Some other terms in Ethiopian cuisine: bederjan (eggplant); doro (chicken); kik (split peas); wot (red pepper sauce); injera (flat pancake like sour bread made from teff flour); teff (a type of grain, can be purchased from PCC).

18425 Pacific Highway South
Sea-Tac, Washington 98188
(Across from the Red Lion Hotel)
(206) 241-5744

Our guests consistently tell us what marvelous aromas we have floating through Sharp's Fresh Roasting. We have three distinct roasters: a real Yakima Fruitwood smoker, a 64 Beam Radiant Roaster, and our temperature-precise Horizontal Spit Roaster.

From these come incomparable whole-natural all white meat turkey breast, what people tell us is the best pork they've eaten, and rich 18 hour flavor cycle sirloin of beef.

And, to finish your meal, we have the world's only genuine Soft Cream. You will have to taste it to believe it.

Jerked Prawns

Serves 4

24 large prawns, shelled and
  cleaned
1 med onion
½ c coarse chopped green onions
2 tsp salt
1 tsp ground allspice

¼ tsp ground nutmeg
½ tsp cinnamon
4 whole jalapeno or serrano
  peppers (remove seeds)
1 tsp ground black pepper

Blend in food processor all ingredients except prawns until smooth. Lay prawns side by side in four groups on a cookie sheet. Spread 1 Tbsp of jerk rub on prawns.

Broil in oven till prawns are done (about 3-4 minutes). Serve with rice.

Two Day Herb Chicken

Serves 2-4

1 3-4 lb fresh chicken
juice of 1 lemon, reserve rind
¼ c olive oil
8 garlic cloves
2 tsp whole basil
2 tsp whole thyme
1 tsp kosher salt

1 tsp brown sugar
1 tsp black pepper, ground
½ c fruitwood wood chips*
1 c water for soaking chips
1 tsp garlic powder
1 tsp onion powder

Day one: mix fruitwood chips, water, onion powder and garlic powder. Cover and let sit.

Combine lemon juice, olive oil, garlic, basil, thyme, brown sugar, salt and pepper in a blender or food processor. Blend until mixture is smooth, about a minute.

Brush chicken liberally, being sure not to neglect the cavity. Put reserved lemon rind in the cavity.

Put the seasoned chicken into a plastic bag, tie the end. Refrigerate.

Day two: light the coals on your Weber BBQ, or any BBQ that has a lid. Remove chicken from the bag. Brush any remaining herb dressing on chicken. When coals are hot, add drained wood chips. Roast chicken at 350-375 degrees on BBQ with lid on for 1½ hours or until hip joint reaches 165 degrees.

*Stop by Sharp's and we'll give you some free!

Sharp's Confetti Salad

Serves 2

1 12-oz head romaine lettuce, cut
   into 1½" by 1½" pieces,
   washed and dried

2 oz sliced mushrooms

4 oz diced tomatoes

1 oz croutons

4 oz blue cheese dressing

8 oz smoked chicken

2 oz sliced black olives

Combine first six ingredients in a salad bowl and gently but thoroughly mix together. Top with chicken and sliced olives.

BLACK ANGUS
Locations in Everett, Bellingham,
Crossroads, Renton, Lynnwood, Yakima, Burien,
Federal Way, Bremerton, and Lakewood.

Stuart Anderson's Black Angus Restaurant has been serving fine steaks, chicken, and seafood all over the Seattle area for 25 years.

Black Bean with Sausage Soup

Makes 10 to 12 gallons

2½ lbs black beans
1¾ gal water
¼ lb ham base
¼ lb chicken base
½ tsp white pepper
couple drops Tabasco
couple drops Worcestershire
1 Tbsp granulated sugar
¼ lb brown sugar
1¼ oz chili powder
½ oz cumin seed

½ tsp oregano
1¼ lb Italian sausage
1 lg onion, diced
5-6 carrots, diced
1 c celery, diced
8 chilis
1-2 med green bell peppers
½ lb bacon fat
½ lb flour
sour cream for garnish

Combine beans, water, ham and chicken bases, white pepper, Tabasco, Worcestershire, sugars, chili powder, cumin and oregano. Bring to boil and simmer until beans are tender, approximately 1 hour.

Chop cooked Italian sausage finely to evenly distribute in soup. Set aside. Add all vegetables to soup. Simmer 15 minutes to cook vegetables. Add sausage.

With bacon fat and flour, make a medium roux. Add to soup in small portions until soup has desired thickness. Dollop sour cream onto each serving.

Chinese Chicken Salad

Serves 1

7 oz mixed salad greens
½ oz carrot, shredded
2 oz bean sprouts, fresh
1 Tbsp red bell pepper, diced
1 tsp sesame seeds, toasted
1 oz cucumber, peeled, ¼" sliced
1 oz chow mein noodles

2 oz salad dressing, sweet & sour
3 leaves flowering kale
4 oz chicken breast, broiled, chilled, cut julienne
1 Tbsp red bell pepper, ¼" diced
1 oz slivered almonds

Gently toss salad greens, carrot, sprouts, pepper, sesame seeds, cucumber and chow mein noodles with salad dressing in a large stainless bowl.

Place salad mixture in bountiful salad bowl. Tuck Kale leaves in back of bowl.

Broil chicken, being careful not to overcook. Chill. Cut like London Broil into strips. Fan and place on top of salad mixture.

Top with additional red pepper and slivered almonds.

Note: canned red bell pepper can be used when the cost of fresh red bell pepper is prohibitive.

Sweet & Sour Ginger Dressing

Makes approximately 1½ cups

2 c granulated sugar

4 tsp dry mustard

1½ c white vinegar

2 Tbsp soy sauce

2 tsp fresh ginger, peeled & grated

1 tsp garlic, minced

¼ c vegetable oil

2 Tbsp sesame oil

2 tsp black pepper

1½ tsp salt

1 Tbsp lemon juice

Sift together sugar and dry mustard. Add vinegar. Cook in a double boiler until sugar dissolves.

Gradually stir in remaining ingredients in order listed. Remove from heat. Refrigerate overnight. Stir well before using.

P.O. Box 532
Sun Valley, Idaho 83353
(208) 622-7124

Sun Valley mustard is a unique product made in Sun Valley, Idaho, containing 100% quality ingredients in five delicious gourmet flavors – Spicy-Sweet, Spicy-Sweet Salt-Free, Chardonnay Wine, Cilantro, and Garlic Rosemary. We are pleased and excited to announce that Sun Valley Chardonnay Wine Mustard recently won the Best New Product Award for 1990-91 by the Idaho Specialty Food Association.

All our gourmet mustards add magic to sandwiches, dips and "dunks," and enhance the flavor of Seafoods, Casseroles, Soups and Sauces, as well as Barbeque Glazes. And added to your favorite Vinegar and Oil mixture or Honey-Yogurt blend, Sun Valley Mustard creates a superb salad dressing.

Sun Valley Mustard is perfect for gifts, and adds excitement to your favorite recipes. Several Gift Packages with recipes and serving suggestions are available.

Salad Dressing

Makes approx. 1½ cups

1 Tbsp Sun Valley Mustard
¼ c vinegar or lemon juice
1½ c vegetable or olive oil

1-2 cloves garlic, chopped
  (optional)
½ tsp paprika (optional)
1 Tbsp honey

Mix together all ingredients and refrigerate.

Creamy Mustard-Honey Dressing

Makes approx. 1½ cups

⅓ c *Sun Valley Mustard*
⅓ c *honey*

½ to ⅔ c *yogurt*
1 to 2 *Tbsp lemon juice*

Whisk together until smooth and creamy. Refrigerate. Serve with fruit salad, spinach, green and cabbage salads.

Mustard Glaze or BBQ Sauce

Makes approx. 1½ cups

½ c Sun Valley Mustard

⅓ c cider vinegar or lemon juice

⅓ c packed light brown sugar

½ c honey

1 Tbsp oriental soy sauce

1 Tbsp oil

Whisk together. Simmer and stir for five minutes. Cool and refrigerate until ready to use (keeps 3 weeks). Great on ribs, lamb and chicken.

Creamy Mustard Baked Chicken

Serves 4-6

4 to 6 chicken breasts
1 c sour cream
1 c chicken stock

3-4 Tbsp Sun Valley Mustard
sprinkle of pepper and nutmeg

Wash and skin chicken breasts. Brown chicken in frying pan briefly. Put chicken in a baking dish.

Mix chicken stock, sour cream, Sun Valley Mustard in a bowl and stir until creamy. Pour mixture over chicken. Sprinkle pepper and nutmeg on top.

Bake at 350 degrees 30-35 minutes. Serve with rice and a garden fresh salad.

Note: Rosemary Garlic Sun Valley Mustard is delightful in this dish.

"HASTA PUEDES TOMAR EL AGUA"

TLAQUEPAQUE Bar

1122 Post Avenue
Seattle, Washington 98101
(206) 467-TACO

In the heart of the Seattle waterfront neighborhood, on the corner of Seneca and Post, lies Tlaquepaque Restaurant and Cantina. Live mariachis, the original tequila "popper," and the only authentic Mexican cuisine in the Northwest, make Tlaquepaque a unique experience. Our original, award winning entrees have captured the attention of the Bite of Seattle judges in years past and this year will be no exception.

Shrimp Mexi-Cone

Serves 2-3

¼ lb shrimp	tortillas
¼ c rice	Jalapeno Glaze ingredients:
¼ c seasoned red beans	1¼ c sugar
¼ c lettuce	1 bell pepper
4 oz salsa	½ c water
2 oz cheese	1¼ diced jalapeno
2 oz sour cream	½ c cilantro vinegar

Combine ingredients for jalapeno glaze in blender and mix until fine. Place mixture in double boiler and cook until all sugar is melted. Saute shrimp in small amount of butter and add enough of jalapeno glaze to coat all of the shrimp. Roll a tortilla in a cone shape and layer the ingredients in the following order form the bottom up: red beans, rice, lettuce, salsa, cheese, sour cream, shrimp. Enjoy!

Variations: for Beef Mexicone, use ½ lb beef skirt, flank. Pound and trim beef skirt until ⅛" thick. Broil with salt, pepper and cayenne for seasoning. Cut into strips or shred. Exclude jalapeno glaze and prepare as above. For Veggie Mexicone: prepare as above, exclude the meat or shrimp.

Fajitas al Mesquite

Serves 2-10

3 lbs unpeeled outside skirt steak
10 whole limes
1 Tbsp garlic salt

1 tsp black pepper
mesquite wood
mesquite charcoal
1 match

Trim skin off of skirt steak and butterfly until paper thin. Cut into thin strips. Cover generously with lime juice, garlic salt, and black pepper. Let marinate overnight.

Broil over mesquite coals. Serve in a hot flour tortilla with hot sauce and pico de gallo relish.

For pico de gallo relish: combine equal amounts of chopped serrano peppers, anaheim peppers, tomato, onion, lime juice, and spices.

Recipe serves 2 to 10 people, depending on how much tequila they have consumed!

Camarones Tocino

Serves 2

12 large prawns
4 whole pickled jalapenos,
  quartered lengthwise

6 bacon strips
butter for deep frying (beer batter
  or your favorite recipe will do)

Split prawns. Stuff with a thin slice of jalapeno and wrap with ½ slice bacon. Put prawns on bamboo skewer (3 to skewer), dip in a beer batter and deep fry.

After frying, baste prawns with a jalapeno and cilantro vinegar sweet and sour sauce. Serve on a bed of rice with a pineapple wedge garnish.

TORAYA TERIYAKI

14339-E NE 20th
Bellevue, Washington 98007
(206) 644-8706

Spring Roll

Serves 2

1½ lb cabbage
½ lb lean beef
6 oz carrot
spring roll wrappers

1½ Tbsp water
1 tsp cornstarch
1 tsp salt
1 tsp corn flour

Shred all ingredients. Season meat with salt and corn flour. Stir fry all ingredients until cabbage is crisp-tender.

Combine 1 Tbsp water, ½ tsp cornstarch and salt. Add to beef mixture and cook till sauce is thickened. Remove from heat and set aside for 1 hour.

Divide beef mixture equally among wrappers. Wrap into small packets, folding and sealing the ends and seams.

Deep fry spring rolls in vegetable oil with temperature around 140 to 150 degrees C. Turn on both sides until each roll is golden brown. Blot excess oil before serving.

Meatball Teriyaki

Serves 2

1 lb lean ground pork

2 tsp sugar

1 Tbsp teriyaki sauce

1 tsp salt

1 tsp cornstarch

2 Tbsp water

Mix all ingredients together. Let stand for 1 hour. Shape into balls. Bake 20 minutes or until browned (350 degree oven). Put on skewers, then grill briefly and serve.

Note: Spring roll wrappers are available in Seattle's International District.

21 Mercer Street
Seattle, Washington
(206) 282-1910

T.S. McHugh's Public House offers a taste of Ireland with fresh baked pot pies from $6.95 and Seattle classics like fresh halibut $13.95 and Caesar salads $5.95, all accompanied with baked on premises Irish Soda Bread. And, of course, made from scratch desserts.

Northwest award-winning wines are served by the glass from $2.95. There are 18 taps pouring Ireland's own Guinness Stout and Harp Lager, along with many of the Northwest's best micro-brews. Featured on the back bar is a fine selection of Irish spirits, from which we pour (at $2.50) Seattle's Best Irish Coffee!

Live sing-a-long Irish music is featured every Friday and Saturday night in the bar. And, in keeping with the Irish tradition, there is of course, no cover charge.

You'll like this place! Hope to see you soon!

T. S. McHugh's **Beef with Guinness Pie**

Serves 6-8

2 lbs lean stewing beef
seasoned flour
3 Tbsp olive oil
3 onions, thinly sliced
2 tsp sugar
1 tsp Colman's mustard
¼ c tomato puree
¼ tsp ground orange peel

bouquet garni (1 bay leaf, 4 parsley stalks, 1 sprig fresh thyme)
20 oz Guinness Stout
8 oz mushrooms
salt
freshly ground pepper
puff pastry sheet, cut into six or eight 4"x4" pieces

Cut beef into 1" cubes. Heat oil in a saucepan at medium-high. Add beef and flour and brown meat on all sides. Remove meat and set aside. Add more oil and saute onions until soft. Deglaze the onion pan with Guinness Stout. Add the sugar, mustard, tomato puree, orange rind, and bouquet garni. Return the meat to the pan. Simmer 2 to 2½ hours or until meat is tender.

Preheat oven to 400 degrees F. Meanwhile, saute the mushrooms in butter for 2-3 minutes and add them to the cooked stew. When the oven is hot, bake the puff pastry squares for 10 minutes or until golden brown.

Dish stew into separate bowls (8 oz portions) and top each with a puff pastry. Serve immediately.

All Irish Reuben Sandwich

Makes 1 sandwich

2 slices rye bread

2 slices Swiss cheese

4 oz eye of corned beef

3 oz fresh sauerkraut*

2 oz Bally Maloe Dressing (Louis or Thousand Island Dressing will work)

Slice corned beef on slicer very thin. Butter 1 side of rye bread and place butter side down on griddle at medium heat. Place 1 slice of Swiss cheese on each slice of bread. Spread corned beef over bread and then top with dressing and sauerkraut.

Cover the sandwich with a lid and let it cook for 10 minutes, or until sandwich is hot and bread is golden brown.

Serve immediately with your favorite chips and dill spears.

*Note: Rinse sauerkraut thoroughly in cold water, then add chicken stock and bacon drippings for flavor.

VALLEY VIEW WINERY

1000 Upper Applegate Road
Jacksonville, Oregon 97530
(503) 899-8468

Stuffed Beef Tenderloin

with Hazelnut Butter & Cabernet Sauce

Serves 4

1 2-lb beef tenderloin
fresh spinach leaves
1 stick unsalted butter, softened
¼ c chopped, toasted hazelnuts
1 Tbsp chopped parsley
1 tsp shallots

Cabernet Sauce:
½ c butter
1 c Mirepoix (mixture of diced onions, carrots, celery)
½ c flour
10 whole black peppercorns
½ c coarsely chopped parsley
6 c beef stock
2 c Valley View Cabernet Sauvignon

For cabernet sauce: melt butter in a heavy saucepan. Add mirepoix and when this begins to brown, add flour. Then add peppercorns and parsley. Stir and mix well, add beef stock and simmer on stove until reduced to the consistency of whipping cream. Keep warm.

Add the wine and reduce again until the consistency of whipping cream.

To assemble tenderloins: butterfly a 2 lb beef tenderloin. Make sure all the fat has been trimmed. Pound with a mallet to flatten slightly. Lay fresh spinach leaves to cover filet, spread liberally with hazelnut butter. Roll filet, tie with string. Brown in small amount of oil. Bake in a 350° oven until beef reaches internal temperature of 125° for medium rare.

To serve, cut string from filet. Slice in 1" slices. Spoon cabernet sauce on plate, place medallion of beef on top of sauce.

* Recipe courtesy of Jacksonville Inn

VIC & MICK'S
NINE-10 CAFE KITCHEN

999 Third Avenue
Seattle, Washington 98104
(206) 622-3999

There are many reasons why Vic & Mick's NINE-10 Cafe has become a reality, but none more important than our desire to serve those whose past and present patronage is the very reason for our existence.

Like virtue, catering to a community's appetite is its own reward. Doing so, in a manner that earns your approval, is the ultimate measure of success. Our hospitality is predicated on the belief that every successful meal requires guests who know what they want, a chef who knows how to prepare it and a manager who understands the meaning of service. Through this blend of under-standing we week to make your dining experience most rewarding for all concerned.

For your convenience we have prepared a balanced, simplified permanent menu. We welcome your suggestions and invite you to make this restaurant your home-away-from-home. It will be our pleasure to see that every reasonable demand is satisfied.

Veal Saltimbocca

Serves 1

3 1½-oz pieces of veal
1½ oz prosciutto ham, sliced
1½ oz mushrooms, sliced
marsala wine

flour
ground sage
1 Tbsp butter

Pound veal into 3 thin portions. Season with sage. Dust lightly with flour. In hot skillet, brown both sides of veal. Put thin slice of prosciutto ham on veal. Add mushrooms and marsala wine. Simmer a few minutes until heated through. Remove veal to heated plate. Reduce sauce until thickened and pour over veal.

Veal Parmigiana

Serves 1

3 1½-oz pieces veal
1 egg, beaten
flour

bread crumbs, seasoned and
  mixed with parmesan cheese
  and chopped parsley
2 slices Jack cheese
tomato sauce, heated

Pound veal thin. Dip in egg, then flour and then in seasoned bread crumbs. In hot skillet, brown both sides of veal. Bake in 350 degree oven for ten minutes. Top with 2 slices of Jack cheese. Put back in oven to melt. Line warm plate with hot tomato sauce. Place veal on top of tomato sauce and serve.

Veal Limone

Serves 1

3 1½-oz pieces veal
flour
butter
olive oil

white wine
lemon juice
splash au jus

Pound veal into 3 thin pieces. Dust lightly with flour. Heat olive oil and butter in skillet. Brown veal on both sides. Add white wine, lemon juice and splash of au jus. Simmer and serve on heated plate.

Semi-Freddo Torte

1 sm pckg pudding mix

1 cup whipping cream

1 cup half and half

1 pound cake, loaf size, sliced horizontally, 3 layers

½ to 1 lb semi-sweet chocolate, finely chopped

½ cup rum

½ cup brandy

1 cup anisette

powdered sugar

cocoa

Combine vanilla pudding mix with whipping cream and half and half. Add finely chopped chocolate.

Combine rum, brandy, and anisette.

Place first layer of cake on serving plate, soak with ⅓ liquor mix. Spread pudding mixture on cake (approximately ½" layer). Repeat layers of pound cake, liquor mix, pudding mixture.

Sprinkle top with mix of powdered sugar and cocoa. Refrigerate at least four hours.

Tortellini a la Vic and Mick's

Serves 8–10

2 lbs tortellini
½ cup butter
½ qt heavy cream
3 oz pesto (or to taste)
¼ cup tomato, skinned &
chopped

sm clove garlic, finely chopped
(optional)
freshly grated parmesan cheese
salt and pepper to taste

To prepare tortellini: bring water to boil in 2-quart saucepan. Add salt. Add pasta slowly, stirring gently to prevent pasta from sticking together. Cook approximately 12–15 minutes. Drain thoroughly.

To prepare sauce: gently saute garlic in a small amount of butter. Add cream and butter. Cook over medium heat until well mixed and it begins reducing. Stir in pesto. Cook over medium heat until desired consistency is reached. Toss in chopped tomatoes just prior to removing from heat.

Mix sauce gently with pasta. Serve hot, sprinkled with parmesan cheese.

Fishermen's Terminal
1735 West Thurman
Seattle, Washington

Chinook's at Salmon Bay offers unique waterfront dining, featuring fresh Northwest seafood at Fishermen's Terminal, home of the Washington and Alaska fishing fleets. The best of each season including such specialties as fresh Alaskan halibut, prized Copper River chinook salmon, Dungeness crab, Northwest oysters, clams, mussels and singing scallops are offered in both traditional and bold, new preparations.

Fishermen's breakfast is served on Saturday and Sunday. Outside deck for warm weather dining! For casual dining, visit "Little Chinook's." Enjoy fish and chips in the heart of Fishermen's Terminal with a view of the fishing fleet.

Old Fashioned
Washington Strawberry Shortcake

Serves 6

2 c flour

2½ Tbsp sugar

⅛ tsp salt

1 Tbsp baking powder

½ c unsalted butter, chilled

¾ c milk

2 c lightly sweetened, lightly whipped cream

3 baskets Washington strawberries, thickly sliced & lightly sweetened

Combine flour, sugar, salt and baking powder in a mixing bowl.

Cut butter into small pieces and rub it into the dry ingredients to form a soft crumble. Stir in the milk until a very soft dough is formed.

Drop six equal portions of dough onto a greased baking sheet. Lightly pat into rounds and brush tops of biscuits with a little cream. Bake at 375 degrees for 12 minutes.

To serve: Split the shortcakes in two, place bottom half of shortcake on a plate and top with sliced berries and a spoonful of whipped cream.

Important: Washington berries give the most juice and the best sweet flavor.

The Third Floor

205 Lake Street
Kirkland, Washington 98033
(206) 822-3553

The 3rd Floor Fish Cafe, located high above Moss Bay in downtown Kirkland, offers the best panoramic waterfront view of any Eastside restaurant. To insure our guests the highest quality Northwest products, the Fish Cafe seasonally adjusts our menus. Please join us for a casual, relaxed dinner, a high powered lunch, or for that special occasion. View banquet facilities for parties up to 32.

Ahi Tuna

with Wasabi Cream Cheese

Serves 4

4 6-oz pieces ahi tuna
seasoned oil for broiling
Wasabi Cream Cheese:
8 oz cream cheese, softened
1 Tbsp soy sauce
1 Tbsp fresh lemon juice

2½ Tbsp wasabi powder (Japanese green horseradish)
2 drops tabasco
½ tsp Sambul Olek (Indonesian red chili sauce)
1 Tbsp brown sugar
2 c minced green onion tops

Blend all Wasabi Cream Cheese ingredients together and mix well. Brush the oil on the tuna and broil to medium rare, about 3 minutes per side.

Top with 2 Tbsp Wasabi Cream Cheese mixture, a sprig of cilantro and a lime wedge to garnish. Service with rice and vegetables.

Sauteed Orange Roughy
with Artichoke & Sundried Tomato Sauce

Serves 4

4 7-oz orange roughy fillets
seasoned flour
2 oz olive oil
6 oz dry white wine
2 Tbsp whole butter
chopped parsley
Sun-Dried Tomato Sauce:
2 oz bacon, diced & cooked crisp
½ red onion, julienne

1 sm jar marinated artichoke hearts
1½ Tbsp Kalamata olives, sliced
1¼ tsp fresh basil
zest of 1 lemon
3 Tbsp sundried tomatoes, diced
4 Tbsp dry white wine
1 Tbsp balsamic vinegar
pinch salt & pepper
1 Tbsp garlic, minced
1 c diced, seeded tomatoes

Artichoke-Sun Dried Tomato Sauce: Simmer all ingredients together until thickened. Let cool.

Dredge fillets lightly in seasoned flour and saute in olive oil until lightly browned, about 2 mintues per side at medium high heat. If necessary, finish cooking in the oven. Keep warm and degrease your pan.

Deglaze pan with white wine and artichoke-sun dried tomato sauce. Cook until almost dry, then fold in whole butter. Serve 3 oz over each fillet. Garnish with a lemon wheel and a pinch of chopped parsley.

from the Kitchens
of
I.P.I. Publishing

Gretchen   Jodd

Steak a la Jood

Serves 4

4 tenderloin steaks
1-2 cloves garlic, crushed

Sauce:
1½ Tbsp Hoisin sauce
½ tsp garlic paste
¼ tsp freshly grated ginger
⅓-½ c soy sauce

Rub fresh garlic on both sides of steaks. Salt and pepper.

Pierce steaks on both sides with sharp fork. Combine all sauce ingredients and baste steaks. Let stand for 10-15 minutes before barbequing.

Cook 8 minutes on first side. Baste, flip and cook another 5-6 minutes.

Serve with baked potatoes and fresh vegetables.

Roasted Pork Loin a la Jood

Serves 4

3-4 lb pork loin

salt

pepper

minced garlic

grey poupon mustard

6 sm red potatoes, quartered

½ white onion

5 fresh carrots, julienne

Baste pork loin with mustard, all sides. Salt, pepper and sprinkle minced garlic to taste.

Bake at 400 degrees for 20-25 minutes per pound.

For vegetables: in an ovenproof baking dish, combine all vegetables. Add ¼ cup water to dish; then salt and pepper vegetables to taste. Put 3-4 Tbsp butter on top of vegetables. Bake covered for ½ hour and uncovered until soft.

Shrimp Enchiladas

Serves 4

Filling:
½ lb bay shrimp
4 Tbsp soft, "light" cream cheese
¼ c sour cream
½ c grated fontina cheese
¼ c grated sharp cheddar cheese
3 Tbsp minced white onion
3 Tbsp minced red bell pepper
freshly ground pepper, to taste
¼ tsp chili powder
¼ tsp dill weed
⅓ of 1 lemon, juiced

8 tortillas
Sauce ingredients:
4 med Roma tomatoes, coarsely chopped
¼ c mild white onion, coarsely chopped
1 Tbsp chopped parsley
¼ tsp salt
½ tsp freshly ground pepper
⅓ c half and half
3 Tbsp "light" cream cheese
⅓ c grated fontina cheese

To prepare enchiladas: combine sour cream and cream cheese, beat with spoon until smooth. Add remaining ingredients. Combine well. Warm tortillas briefly to soften. On center of each tortilla, place about 3 Tbsp mixture. Roll up to enclose filling.

To prepare sauce: heat half and half with cream cheese until cream cheese is melted.

Combine tomatoes, onion, salt, pepper and parsley in small bowl.

To assemble: lightly oil a shallow casserole large enough to hold enchiladas in one layer. Pour a little of the cream cheese sauce in bottom of casserole. Place enchiladas in casserole. Pour remaining cream cheese sauce over enchiladas. Cover with tomatoes and sprinkle grated cheese over tomatoes. Bake at 475 degrees for 10 to 12 minutes, until filling is hot and bubbling.

Note: the shrimp filling is equally good used cold, as a filling for avocados, sandwiches, etc.

Hot Artichoke Dip

4 oz cream cheese

2 oz blue cheese

1 sm jar marinated artichoke
   hearts, chopped coarsely

¾ c sour cream

½ c mayonnaise

½ c parmesan

1½ c shredded spinach

¼ c chopped onions, red pepper

1 Tbsp oil

pepper to taste

¼ c sliced almonds

1 Tbsp green onion tops, chopped

Heat oil in small pan. Saute onion and pepper until onion is soft. Add spinach and cook 2-3 minutes. Add artichoke hearts. Remove from heat.

Combine softened cream cheese with blue cheese. Add spinach mixture, sour cream and mayonnaise.

Heat oven to 375 degrees. Pour mixture into shallow 6-8" casserole. Sprinkle with almonds and green onions. Bake in 400 degree oven until bubbling. Serve hot with crackers, thinly sliced French or rye bread, etc.

A

W

Z

Kitchen Notes:

WANT YOUR COOKING TO GET RAVE REVIEWS?

GIVE IT THE
FIVE-STAR TREATMENT.

At our Five-Star Kitchen, we can equip you
with top-name gourmet cookware, cutlery and
state-of-the-art electrics. And since presentation counts
too, check out our colorful dinnerware and serveware.
Stop by any of our stores today, and from now on
every meal can be a five-star event.

☆ **Belgique** ☆ **Chicago**☆ **Revere**☆ **Corning**
☆ **Circulon** ☆ **Calphalon** ☆ **Pfaltzgraff**
☆ **Luigi Bormioli** ☆ **Oneida**☆ **Braun** ☆ **Krups**
☆ **KitchenAid** ☆ **Cuisinart**

The **BON** MARCHÉ

Tables of Equivalents

WEIGHTS & MEASURES

60 drops . . . . 1 teaspoon
3 teaspoons . . . . 1 tablespoon
2 tablespoons . . . . . 1 liquid ounce
4 tablespoons . . . . ¼ cup
16 tablespoons . . . . 1 cup
2 cups . . . . 1 pint
2 pints . . . . 1 quart
4 quarts . . . . 1 gallon
8 quarts . . . . 1 peck
4 pecks . . . . 1 bushel
16 ounces . . . . = 1 pound

EGG

8 to 10 egg whites . . . . 1 cup
10 to 14 egg yolks . . . . 1 cup
4 to 6 whole eggs . . . . 1 cup

COCOA & CHOCOLATE

For 1 ounce (square) chocolate use

4 tablespoons cocoa and ½ tablespoon fat.

For ¼ cup or 4 tablespoons cocoa use 1 ounce (square) chocolate and omit ½ tablespoon fat.

GENERAL EQUIVALENTS

2 cups solid butter = 1 pound
1 bouillon cube = 1 teaspoon beef extract
1 tablespoon cornstarch = ⅔ tablespoon arrowroot or 1¼ tablespoons wheat or rice flour
1 tablespoon unflavored gelatin = ¼ ounce (or 2⅔ leaves leaf or French gelatin)

FRESH FRUIT

1 pound apples . . . . 2 to 6 apples: 3 cups, diced; 1½ cups sauce
1 pound apricots . . . . 8 to 14 apricots; about 2½ cups, cooked
1 medium avocado . . . . about 2 cups, cubed
1 pound bananas . . . . about 3 bananas; about 2 cups, sliced
1 pint berries . . . . about 2 cups
1 pound cherries . . . . 3 cups, stemmed; about 2½ cups, pitted
1 pound cranberries . . . . about 4 cups; about 4 cups sauce
1 medium grapefruit . . . . about 1⅓ cups pulp, about 1 cup juice
1 pound grapes . . . . about 1 bunch; about 2 cups, halved
1 dozen lemons . . . . about 2½ cups juice
1 dozen oranges . . . . 3 to 5 cups juice
1 pound peaches . . . . 4 to 6 peaches; about 2½ cups, sliced
1 pound pears . . . . 3 to 5 pears; about 2½ cups, cooked
1 pineapple . . . . about 2½ cups, cubed
1 pound plums . . . . 12 to 20 plums; about 2 cups, cooked
1 pound rhubarb . . . . 4 to 8 stalks; 3½ cups diced; 2 cups, cooked

I.P.I. Publishing
10245 Main Street, Suite 8-3
Bellevue, Washington 98004
(206) 454-8473

Please send me_____copies of **The Bite of Seattle Cookbook** at $12.95 each (plus $1.04
sales tax [Wash. residents] and $2.00 postage and handling: Total $15.99)

Enclosed is my check for $_____.

Name_____

Address_____

City_____State_____Zip_____

☐ This is a gift. Send directly to:

Name_____

Address_____

City_____State_____Zip_____

– (Cut Here) --

I.P.I. Publishing
10245 Main Street, Suite 8-3
Bellevue, Washington 98004
(206) 454-8473

Please send me_____copies of **The Bite of Seattle Cookbook** at $12.95 each (plus $1.04
sales tax [Wash. residents] and $2.00 postage and handling: Total $15.99)

Enclosed is my check for $_____.

Name_____

Address_____

City_____State_____Zip_____

☐ This is a gift. Send directly to:

Name_____

Address_____

City_____State_____Zip_____

Kitchen Notes: